AF291363

Listen to My Heart

A Repertoire of Poetry
by Christian Authors

Selected Works By

KATRINA WALLACE

authorHOUSE

AuthorHouse™
1663 Liberty Drive
Bloomington, IN 47403
www.authorhouse.com
Phone: 1 (800) 839-8640

Published by AuthorHouse 09/22/2015

ISBN: 978-1-5049-4872-2 (sc)
ISBN: 978-1-5049-4873-9 (e)

Library of Congress Control Number: 2015914528

Print information available on the last page.

This book is printed on acid-free paper.

CONTENTS

FOREWORD

One of the joys of serving as Pastor for over twenty-six years has been the relationships I have developed with some of God's finest people. The persons who have contributed to this book are among that group. The passion and devotion to God in spreading His love is the motivation and driving force behind this work. As you read the various contributions, you will be taken into some of the most creative and intriguing minds in the Body of Christ. You will get more than merely literary compositions and poems; you will get a glimpse into the pure and sincere spirit of those who God has chosen to use for His glory. As you enjoy reading these selections, you may not even notice how powerful they are in lifting your spirit and giving you a boost. I hope this is the first of many more books by these same individuals because clearly there is more where this has come from. I am grateful to God that He is moving beyond the traditional ways the gospel is communicated and distributed out in forms like this. I am certain you will be blessed by this work and pray that you will be so inclined to share it with others.

Rev. Daniel T. Mangrum, Pastor
Cornerstone Peaceful Bible Baptist Church
Upper Marlboro, Maryland

INTRODUCTION

Listen to My Heart Speak is a compilation of poetic letters written by writers from different walks of life. Candidly and vividly, lyricists open their hearts on paper describing the metamorphosis of a sometimes ailing soul as it goes through renewal until a fully delivered spirit is born. Feelings, desires, and beliefs are poetically exhaled as the process of writing brings forth hope, victory, and deliverance. This is the Psalm of our generation.

This book is written to encourage and to liberate those who know our struggle, because it is or has been their struggle. It's written to empower people who are bottled up, but can't put their feelings into words that so desperately need to be released. It's written for all lovers of poetry that can appreciate and dance to the beat of our hearts as we reveal our life experiences in words.

There are times when we were afraid and times when we were boldly confident. Read it and see for yourselves how poetically we have written our way to freedom. It has been a remarkable journey in which we've grown and still…our best is yet to come.

PREFACE

The Poet Who Writes, But Is Seldom Heard

© 2010 Talaya Simpson

I am the poet who writes, but is seldom heard.

Mouth covered with cotton filled verbs like …

    can't

        maybe

            won't

And sealed up with phrases like … if you do, what if they don't

    Like

        Appreciate

            Care or understand

And forever will you remain the poet who writes, but is seldom heard
Because you share only a

    little,

        teeny,

            tiny word.

One that is safe and accepted.

Poet! I hear you crying.

Poet! I hear your voice scream as loud as a siren, when a tornado blows
  … as loud as a train, when it goes by the station without stopping full
  speed.

A cry so loud, it can only be heard by those whose ears
  are tuned to the pain for they are one and the same.

    … Poets who write, but are seldom heard.

I've come to awaken you and to give you release.
Your voice must be heard.
It's the only means to your peace.

Open your book. Let loose your pen.
You're not holding people out … you're caging yourself in!

There's a voice missing in the wilderness
that brings life to those whose cadence
was meant to blend with the pen God gave YOU …

Please let them in, Poet.

  Open up, Poet.

    Share Poet.

For you are

P … POISED TO
O … OFFER
E … EVERYTHING GOD HAS MADE
T … THROUGH YOU!

For you are free …

    now …

      be …

        HEARD!

ONE

My Heart's Cry

My Heart's Cry was the original title of the poem "Who am I." This was the first writing that came at a time in my life when I was discovering who I was and learning to appreciate my uniqueness. For so long, I defined myself by relationships and accomplishments. However, it was this writing that marked the beginning of poetic expressions and redefined what "self-awareness" meant to me. Through this journey, I learned who I was and what I liked. Writing helped me to get in touch with my own feelings, desires, fears, hurts, and insecurities, resulting in the healing process of a girl whose self-esteem was critically wounded. All of the writings in this chapter are a cry from my heart while I was either single or married. Although my life had been illuminated when I began to write, it was still a very dark time. Writing helped me to crawl, walk, sometimes stagger, and even run through the darkness while I reached for the One who illuminated and reconstructed me at the very core of my being. Through this my existence became meaningful, my worth was validated, and my once angry and fretful heart was healed.

Enjoy!

Katrina L. Harrell-Wallace

WHO AM I?

WHO AM I?

I am a *BLACK WOMAN*, a black virtuous woman who loves being a woman who can look in the mirror and behold the beauty of my blackness, because my blackness is beautiful. I am a spirit, a soul-being, and my personality and the way that I am is my character (my inner-woman). It's my inner-woman that makes me who I am: different, unique, unlike any other woman.

Hmmm, I think and I wonder...Who am I? ***Who am I?*** I am a child of the most High God, a new creation in Christ Jesus, girded with strength and honor. A woman who is not perfect, but being made perfect daily by the Word of God and the yielding of my will to God's will and His Holy Spirit.

WHAT DO I DESIRE?

My desires are to remain a God-fearing woman, to be a good wife doing my husband well always, and to be a blessed mother. I desire to love and to be loved, to give and to be used by God to be a blessing to someone else. I want to grow in God and be the best that I can be in every area of my life.

It is ***not*** my desire to hate, be envious, or jealous of people. I do ***not*** want to be judgmental, and when I get married, I ***definitely*** don't want a wimp for a husband. The man that I pray for (my soulmate, my spirit to spirit) is a man whose inner-man is born again as well. I want a New Creation, who is being renewed by the word of God and transformed in the image of God. I want a man who knows the Lord for himself and loves the Lord, because then and only then will he know how to love me. I want a man who's gentle, warm, giving, caring, loving, sharing, understanding, and fun; yet, he should also be strong and wise. I want a man who can truly be the priest of our house: a mature man who is open and honest, and one who is a good example and father for our children; a man who is faithful to his calling by God, because only then can he also be faithful to me.

WHAT CAN I OFFER?

I can love, for GOD has taught me real love and is perfecting it daily. I can be his comfort, support, and warmth when he needs someone there. I can be encouragement because I know who our help is, the sister when he needs a friend, the shoulder to cry on, and a listener when he wants to talk; but let's not forget that I can never be a substitute in the place where God should be in his life. So in the event that I am not around, he needs to know the Lord. God has to be in his life! What else can I offer? Well, I offer prayer. I know who to pray to and I know that *my* GOD is faithful!

WHO AM I?

I am a *BLACK WOMAN* who is beautiful, not said in conceit, but because I am a creation of GOD.

By Katrina L. Harrell

ARE YOU THE ONE?

Are you the one?
Or is there another?
Don't waste my time.
Don't play with me, brother.

I'm on a mission
Need to know if you're sincere.
I can't mess around
I must keep my head clear so I may truly hear.

My guards are up.
That's just the way it has to be.
Only God, my Father, can confirm
Your value, worth, and importance to me.

Don't even try to tell me,
The "God told me you're my wife" bit
When I speak to Him every day.
Be clear that I'm not falling for the lame and foolish pitch.

So come correct
And let me just set the record straight,
There will be no free sampling.
It's been YEEAARSS since Ms. Kitty has had any ac-tiv-i-tay.

I will not be your ego mission.
You will not bring me down!
Get this: "I refuse to play with fire."
So on days when she purrs: it's in prayer that I am found.

I'll call on the Lord until He comes through.
I'll speak to my flesh and command her to obey.
I'll lock myself in my room if I have to.
"You are NOT in charge!" I will say.

It is my earnest desire
Not to hurt God or let Him down.
He's been so loving and kind to me;
I refuse to fool around.

I'm waiting for the real McCoy, my Isaac;
Do you hear?
So get to stepping if you're not the one.
I have **No** time for crumbs, my dear.

So come correct, my brother.
That's all I have to say.
I'm a refined sista with no time for junk
I'm saving my pearls and doing it God's way!

By Katrina L. Harrell

A New and Better ME

I know to most I appear strong,
But I'm really fragile on the inside.
There have been so many disappointments encountered;
It's hard to trust people and believe me I've tried.

It's not all because of others
That I am of a distrusting way.
I know how I once was
Before God changed me and had His say.

I tried to be straight up in relationships.
I forewarned brothers how the relationship would be.
I had grown hard and callous by life's experiences.
You had to be strong and have backbone to deal with me.

But God would take a relationship
To break me down inside;
To teach me how I hurt people
And for 3 years, He chastised me to deliver me from pride.

My heart was painfully sorrowful.
My flesh was being crucified.
I hated the years of constant surgeries,
But He was determined to make me a worthy bride.

I thought it would never be over.
I cried, "God, how long will You buffet me?"
He replied, "You've come a long way, my daughter,
But it's not over until I've changed you completely."

It was three years before the trial ended,
But the process seemed like an eternity.
Although it was painful going through it,
I'm thankful because it made me **A Better Me!**

By Katrina L. Harrell

IS THERE A MAN QUALIFIED?

Is there a man who can love a GOD-fearing woman like me?
Is there a Hu-man, who can cherish me as a gift of
GOD, who will respect me as a woman of God and
appreciate my love for that which is holy?

Is there one that can truly love me like Christ loves the church?
According to God's will and commandment;
one who truly honors His precepts,
Values, and appreciates my worth.

Is there a man who has a mind of his own?
A man who's not easily influenced by the ignorance of the
ignorant, but who's influenced by God's righteousness, truth
and who likewise wants the blessedness of a happy home.

Is there one who's tired of playing games?
But who's ready to be serious, responsible, and committed…
Not one who's looking to fulfill his Own needs,
speaking gibberish, and making foolish claims.

Is there one who can handle the woman that God has made me to be?
Is there one who's honest, sincere, and not
selfishly thinking of only himself,
But who can love me until I depart into my eternity?

Is there a man who's ready, willing, and able?
A man who gets satisfaction at working to develop and maintain
a healthy relationship; a GODLY man who can communicate
without it just being about sex and who honors the Bible.

You see, my prayer is for a real man;
Not just that which separates male from a female or a shell of a
man with no substance inside. I'm speaking of that which makes
a man wise, according to GOD's definition of a Godly man.

Is there a man who will respect my body as something
sacred like the temple of God that I am?
A man striving to be better for GOD and
working at doing what's best for us;
Who's not egotistical, but loves me with a
love like unto the sacrificial lamb.

Is there one who will take time to listen, even
if the voice is that of a woman?
Is there one who's not operating solely on his strength,
but who's secure knowing that being Gentle (in the right
context) is a strength that makes him a worthy man?

Is there one who realizes that being honest is the
perfect foundation for a relationship?
That being loving and apologetic doesn't diminish masculinity and
Who can deal with a strong black woman and not trip.

Is there a man who thinks like me?
Who believes that a relationship needs to have quality
time set aside to experience one another…
That couples should talk, share, encourage each
other and pray for one another…
And be first to each other after God, even above his own mother?

So again, is there a man who understands, agrees,
and wants this in their relationship to be?
Is there a man who will work and commit himself in his relationship?
GOD, is there a man for me?

By Katrina L. Harrell

KNOCK KNOCK

Knock, Knock…Who's there?
Let me in, I want to be your friend.
Why is it that you won't let your guards down?
Why have you barricaded yourself in?
    I've told you that I can't trust you.
    "That" you have proven to me.
    Through careful observation,
    You're not trustworthy from what I can see.
So even though you wish
To become my friend and be close to me,
I'm sorry but this is
The most that you can or ever will be.
    They say rejected people reject people.
    I can conclude that sometimes that is true.
    You believe that it's my issues;
    That's keeping me from drawing close to you.
But rejection is not my issue this time;
It's deeper than that for me.
It's the vibes that I pick up from your spirit
That just doesn't sit well with me.
    It's the venom in your spirit.
    The green monster that you think is me.
    You are deceived by your own wickedness
    And that's the barrier that I perceive and see.
I pray for you my sister
And I pray for my spirit too.
I want God's best for everyone,
But right now, more specifically you.
    There's manipulation in your ways
    And your motives are filled with selfishness.
    You're not genuine or sincere.
    You serve yourself without consciousness.

You are extremely narcissistic
And it's all about accommodating you.
I can't and won't nurture your character flaws.
So as it relates to you, being cordial is all I can do.

By Katrina L. Wallace

Death of Self

I pledge my love to You,
Submit to do whatever You ask me to.
I yield my will to Your will for me..
I will be who You've said I will be
I will comply with that which You have spoken over me.
I will surrender my all to Your plan.

I've learned to trust You and always obey.
Although it hasn't been easy, I'd rather do it Your way.
Your way is perfect and better than mine could ever be,
Because You always work in the best interest of me.
And most of all, You help me to grow internally.
Therefore, I yield like putty in Your Hands.

Oftentimes I don't understand it (Your way) and it doesn't feel good,
But with all that is within me, I will surrender to do as I should.
So I pledge myself to You today,
To be a vessel that will bring You glory because I've chosen Your way.
For "obedience is better than sacrifice," You say.
My very life I place into Your hands.

I offer, I surrender, I submit,
I give, I yield, I commit,
Everything to You.
It's the least that I can do.
I resist my will; die to my flesh because I really do want You.
I trust in the wisdom of Your master plan.

I pledge my love to You today,
For how could I say I love You and not do the things You say?
If I truly love You then I would just trust and obey.
So with my whole heart, I commit myself to Your way.
I give You back this life, this life that's not my own.
I die to self to follow after You, because it's to You that I belong.

Not my will, but Thy will be done.
This is the example of Your dear and precious Son;
He taught us to die to self, crucify our flesh daily.
This is the path to having and showing His Glory.
So I will follow after the Spirit and not after the flesh.
I die daily until there is no more of me left.

By Katrina L. Wallace

I'm a Princess!

I'm a Princess!
That's what my mother says to me.
A beautiful honey golden princess,
Gorgeous as I can be.

She always says, "Hold your head up!"
And "Lift your countenance too."
People may have their opinions,
But it's not what they think; it's what *you* think of you.

Beauty is not just how you look,
It's who you are inside.
Take special care to nurture the inner you
And let integrity be your guide.

Princess, my little princess,
Be the best that you can be.
Be grateful for your talents and
Take advantage of every God-given opportunity.

Opportunities to learn
Opportunities to grow
Opportunities to shine
And let your giftedness show.

Opportunities to give
Opportunities to pray
Opportunities to celebrate
Remembering Christ gives you *each day*.

You're a princess, my daughter.
This is not something I would vainly say.
It's imperative that you embrace who you are
And let no one steer you away.

Hold your head up, princess.
You are fearfully and wonderfully made!
Have confidence in how God has created you
Because God doesn't make junk or mistakes.

You're an over-comer, you're victorious,
And you have been divinely set apart.
Even though all your days may not be happy ones,
Keep Jesus in your heart.

Speak life and choose life.
That's what the Bible tells us to do.
There are effects and consequences in your choices,
So please give thought to what you choose.

Always remember you are destined.
You have a purpose and God has a plan for you.
Trust in Him always, because when you trust in God,
There's nothing that you can't do.

By Katrina L. Wallace

My Father is the King!

My Father is the King.
He's ruler of everything.
It is because of my Father that I am royalty;
A pearl of great price is what He thinks of me.

Royal blood running through my veins,
Born with an advantage because of His fame.
There's nothing that I can't accomplish in His name,
So why should I ever doubt or be dismayed?

There's a rich inheritance for being a child of the King,
That's why I'm so glad to be a part of this family.
Who would've ever thought I'd be blessed to this degree?
My Abba Father knew, because it was He who destined me to be.

My Daddy is the King,
So what does that make me?
Privileged to be born into this family of Royalty,
Blessed and highly favored, living a life of opportunity.

It is because of my relationship with the King
That I have peace, even in adversity.
I have His favor, but it's not just for me.
You can accept this inheritance, if you would just trust and believe.

God is real, as real as "real" can be.
I know, because He is real inside of me.
My experiences in life bear witness that He is true.
I just pray that you come to know Him and love Him as I do.

Jehovah IS the King,
Ruler of Everything.
He's my Abba Father,
Which makes me an heir of His Majesty!

By Katrina L.Wallace

Freed to Love

Guarded

Suspicious

Who can trust being in a relationship?

Fearful

Apprehensive

Questioning every intention, because fear has such a strong grip.

Should I let my guard down?
NO! Because I am afraid,
But don't know why.

Is he a wolf in sheep's clothing?
Can he be trusted?
These are the questions that bombard my mind.

I cried unto the Lord,
"Please help me!"
Lead me Father because I'm confused.

I don't trust my own judgment
And I will not move
Until I know You approve.

I only want Your best for me.
I'll remain still until I receive
Your peace and absolute clarity.

Then my God spoke to me:
"Renounce the fears
And accept My liberty.

There is no need for you to fear.
Accept My peace
And to Me draw near.

Renounce your fears,
For this is in accordance with My plan.
You're snared and it's 'suspicion' that's the strongman."

So I renounced my fears, Yes I Did!
Called them out, till I was free.
It was such a good feeling to have those bondages off of me.

Now, I'm freed to Love.
Yes, Your love has liberated me.
I thank You, God, for Your Word and I trust now even more completely.

By Katrina L. Harrell

Life Poured Out

Many girls are hurting,
Confused as they can be.
Dealing with life's crises,
Struggling to find their true identity.

Self-absorbed I can't be,
Thinking about only what will make me happy.
When my sister's ways scream, **"I'm hurting!"**
How could I pray and think of what will satisfy only me?

To step outside myself,
To get rid of all that is of me,
To climb into Your will, Father,
So that You can use me as a Blessing.

To free myself from the need for more,
When so many struggle and are poor.
Poor in spirit and destitute within,
What can I do to swing open their door?

What can I render and sacrifice
So that others may be free?
One thing is for certain and that is
It will never happen if my life is just about "me."

That door that gives way
To heal their soul.
Their minds that have grown weary,
Their hearts that have become cold.

Their cries that have dried from their faces
And the screams that are no longer heard.
What can I do Father to make a difference in their lives?
I can offer myself and share Your Word.

It's not about me,
But it's about the girl I used to be,
That still exists in many girls around me.
So I empty myself of "me" and surrender my life to be an offering.

By Katrina L. Wallace

Will I survive?

So many things going on in my head:
The constant agony of my mother's dread,
The insecurity, instability, the fragility of my atmosphere makes me mad,
The rage that's perpetuated by my present, but absent Dad.

Will I survive?

So I drank and I smoked drugs trying to numb the pain.
Sometimes I thought I was going insane.
Oh, how I wish to escape this bad dream that torments my mind.
Constantly asking myself the question, "Lord, Why?"

How could he treat me with such dis-regard?
Why does my mother stay? I **reeeally** don't understand this part.
Why is it that my life is messed up in this way?
I wish that all this pain would just go away.

Will I survive?

I hate to see her accept her life as it is.
She deserves better, yet she continues to settle for this.
I wish she understood her own value and worth.
No woman deserves to be disrespected or treated like dirt.

Yet she remains and this just frustrates me.
Even drinking and sex won't let me out of this reality.
The drugs don't numb me like I thought they would,
They just cause me to think harder and fuel the hate, overtaking my childhood.

I wish to end it all, one of us has to go.
If he remains, then I'll just have to put an end to this dysfunctional, painful show.
But as much as I contemplate death, I'm too conscious of God and He won't let me be.
I've been close, ever so close, but never had the guts to take my life prematurely.

Did I survive?

More than 2 decades later,
I look back on this time for me.
I'm happy to have survived it,
Although, I never thought I'd see

The day that my natural father and I would dwell as a happy family,
Me loving him and him loving me.
It's an incredible testimony to God's abilities.
Who would have ever thought this would ever be?

I did survive…I did survive.
I became the victor and have been healed from this awful pain.
God delivered me from all the hurt, hate and shame,
But the greatest of all is this: He saved my father's soul by His WONDERFUL LOVING GRACE.
And He continues to make my mom, daddy, and I whole.

By Katrina L. Harrell

Self

Here I was trying hard to concentrate, yet no matter how hard I tried to focus, I kept getting distracted by my affliction. I heard the pastor speaking but my attention was overpowered by my imperfections, and although I tried to listen, I couldn't because I was too self-conscious.

Then something happened. I was separated from myself in the spirit.
I saw myself left sitting there in my seat. Service was still going on, but I was no longer conscious of me because I had been separated from me. The cares, the concerns, and the fears were all left with my flesh.

It then became easier to look, listen, and concentrate on God. I was no longer distracted
with myself, but focused on Him. I was no longer self-conscious, but God-conscious.
God became the object of my attention, because I was no longer **In the Way.**

Liberated in that moment in time from what people thought, how I looked, and my flaws,
I realized that I was the hindrance to my relationship with God. I couldn't hear Him fully on that day, because I was heavy on my own mind. Separated from myself, I was right where God wanted me to be.

"I'm sorry," my soul screamed loudly within. I'm sooo sorry that I let myself get in the way of pure, intentional, and focused worship. I *did* worship You with my mouth, but my heart was far from You. I even looked as if I was listening by my body language and appeared to be in tune, but my heart and my mind was divided. My focus was more on me than You. I identified the struggle, but didn't challenge my thoughts to obey what was more important.

My issues were so small, but I allowed them to be magnified. I surrendered to myself instead of submitting to YOU. You are so much bigger than any of my problems. You are so much greater than any of my flaws. I repent that I allowed myself to become a god worthy of my mental devotion instead of focusing on the One who's the only wise God.

Yes Lord, yes Daddy…how can I serve You? I'm listening. You have my complete attention. I cease to exist and it is You that is my Everything. You are my ALL and ALL. It is You that deserves my complete and total devotion.

After my submission, I experienced His peace. There was such a calmness. **Time Stood Still** and I could hear God clearly say, "Be still and set your affections on Me. I could not talk with you because you were too self-conscious, but now that I have your attention: listen my daughter and look to ME, your Abba Father. I am your peace. I am your peace. Quiet your mind and rest in Me, because I am your rest. I am your healer, and I am your sustainer. I am your deliverer; I am your ALL and ALL."

Then softly, but with much emotion my response was, "Yes Lord…My soul says yes! You are my All and All!"

By Katrina L. Wallace

Unstoppable!

You can't stop me.
You can't oppress me.
You can't bind me
Or hold me down.
    You can't manipulate me.
    You won't weaken me.
    You won't confuse me
    Nor will you turn my smile into a frown.
You won't destroy me.
You won't distract me.
You won't snare me
Nor keep me from fulfilling God's plan for my life.
    You can't deny me.
    You can't shut me down in the Spirit.
    You won't deflate me
    Or cause me to walk in strife.
You are deceived to think that you can hinder
What God is doing in me.
To even assume that you can impede me
Is a waste of your time and energy.
    You can gather a counsel against me.
    You can conspire to ostracize me too.
    You can sow evil seeds of discord,
    Using cunning manipulation, deception, or even voodoo.
I will still rise above your foolishness,
While all along you're hating on me
Because you cannot hinder, my friend,
God's purpose and plan for whom and what I shall be.
    I will rise above hypocrisy
    And your evil plot to make me look bad.
    I will rise even in adversity,
    Because I already have.

I've decided to take the high road
And set my affection on things above.
I've learned to escape into the resting place
Of my Savior, my Friend, and my Love.

By Katrina L. Wallace

Running Scared

Heart palpitating, breathing uncontrollably,
Thoughts racing through my head.
He was right behind me, waiting for me to open the door.
No! I can't open it. If I do, then I'm sure my mother would find me dead.

Every day when I came home from school,
I felt him watching me, staring intently as I passed by.
If only someone would have listened to me.
I warned them. Yes, I tried to be heard, but no one would hear my cry.

I was extremely terrified.
What should I do? I *do* not know.
This can't be happening; I'm just a little girl.
This is not the way I wanted to go.

Crying and screaming frantically,
Yell girl! Yell! Yell as loud as you can.
Shaking like a leaf, I think….God please help me!
Please save me from this man!

My heart is still pounding.
With terror in my eyes, I ask can anyone hear.
Thank Goodness, thank goodness, could it be that he ran off on his own!
I'm still shaking, yet I don't see him. God, did You make him disappear?

Safe now that I'm in my house,
But still delirious, I don't know what I am to do.
Panic-stricken I run back and forth, hyperventilating.
I grab and cling to a family feud game; I would have fainted had anyone
just whispered, "Boo!"

So I run! I run out the back door…I jet.
I run as fast as I can,
But who do I see when I run out the back door?
Oh No! It's him…It's him all over again!

I dashed by him, almost knocked him over.
I didn't even lock my back door.
If I could just get to a friend's house,
I will never walk home alone anymore.

Every day thereafter, I was afraid
And my fear just grew and grew.
I hated being a latchkey kid,
But what was a young poor little girl to do?

By Katrina L. Harrell

I NEED YOU!

Abba Father,
Please breathe on me today.
I need to feel the cool wind of Your comfort
That reassures me that everything will be okay.

I'm relieved of my stress
And my worries fade away.
In the fellowship of Your embrace,
Do I find solitude to break up my hectic day.

Curled up in Your lap,
Snuggled so very closely.
What peace my soul experiences
When I'm inhaling life from Your Glory.

To close my eyes
And release a deep long sigh,
To forget about all of life's ties
And to rest, still and safely below Your eyes.

Father, I need a kiss
And a touch from You today.
I need to dwell alone with You, Daddy,
Just You and I fellowshipping for as long as I can stay.

By Katrina L. Wallace

Happy to be "ME"

I am who I am,
That's all I can be.
I'm tired of being frustrated,
Trying to be someone other than who I was meant to be.

My voice is my voice.
My speech is my speech.
My talents are my talents.
My style, looks, and personality are original…I should be grateful for each.

Still I struggle to feel content
With the person that I am.
I must free myself
Of this internal conflict, foolish strivings, and bedlam.

How will I ever
Feel adequate inside
If I'm always comparing myself,
Admiring the qualities of others, and tossing my attributes aside?

Stop! Come to Yourself, Girl!
You are one of a kind.
You have your own beautiful qualities
That you should be happy to say, "Are all mine."

No matter what gifts I don't possess,
I have a reason to be "Happy To Be Me."
God has created me as a Masterpiece
When He took care to create and package the persona of me.

So why would I waste my time
Trying to be a duplicate of someone else's being,
When I can be the original, creative, and imaginative person that I am,
Satisfied and content with my own wellbeing?

By Katrina L. Wallace

What's Important Now

As boys we all dreamed of what we would be,
Locked in on some dream or vision we could see.
Shaped by our environment and media influence,
We wanted to reach some level of prominence and affluence.

But as life evolved, many things shaped the process.
There were many twists and turns, and our dreams were put to the test.
Most of us did not become what we had thought.
What we ended up with was not what we sought.

At some point, we realized those things were just dreams
And life does not always appear as it seems.
We did not become all we had hoped we would become one day;
Things did not turn out in the most ideal way.

We did not become the next Michael Jordon in basketball;
We just couldn't jump as high and we didn't grow that tall.
We didn't become the next Marvin Gaye at the top of the charts,
Singing before adoring fans, breaking young girls' hearts.

We did not become the next Muhammad Ali,
Floating like a butterfly and stinging like a bee.
We couldn't take a punch and our jab was weak,
Surviving a fight in grade school was our boxing career peak.

Let's face it…we did not become the next great star in lights,
Making headlines, doing interviews and reaching to great heights.
Our names are not going to be in any Hall of fame.
We don't have any asterisks or special mention by our name.

But I am not disappointed, I would not change a thing,
I have learned to appreciate whatever life may bring.
I have learned that all those dreams I was counting
Were really unreal and not at all important.
As I approach 50, my perspective is drastically changed.
The way I look at things has been totally rearranged.
I realize as I approach a little past my prime,
That what the world values is really a waste of time.

Of all the pursuits, parenting is the closest to reality,
The opportunity to pass on immortality,
A chance to impact future generations of the human race,
And leave a legacy that will make this world a better place.

I realize a lot of things were really about myself,
Attaining worldly possessions and personal wealth.
All of which will go to someone else when I die.
At the end I will be left empty, vain and dry.
But what I put in my children is the only thing that will last.
I will continue to live long after this life has past.
All this running around trying to save the world
Is not as important and being there for my baby girl.

And so I have made some choices and priorities diverted,
I have experienced a change, repented, and in a way been converted.
The world has its own definition of true success.
It has criteria you must meet in order to be considered the best.
But my goal is not about any of those goals or objective,
I have experienced a metamorphosis, a transformation in perspective.

I would rather be there from my daughter than have my name in lights,
Than having some trophy, or personal accomplishment in my sights.
I would rather have her know me than be known by a great crowd.
I would rather be her hero and the one for which she is proud.

I would rather be the one who is her special friend.
When she has a problem, the one on whom she can depend.
I would rather be in a relationship with her, in which we share a lot,
That is enduring all the way to adulthood from the time she was a tot.

I would rather be at her graduation than accepting some award,
Being there for her is the best that life can afford.
I would rather be helping her with her homework and taking her to school,
Than out hanging out, trying to be a player and acting like a fool.

It is more important to me that I am there when she goes through her stuff,
When life throws her a curve and things start to get rough.
I want to be there when she experiences her first heartbreak
Or when she makes her first great mistake.

I want to be there when she needs some support and concern,
When at the foot of adversity she has to grow and learn.
My prayer is that I not be so caught up in what I can boast,
That I fail to be there for her when she needs me the most.

When it is my time to go and breathe my last breath,
I hope the most valuable thing that I would have left
Is a life dedicated to her in all I did, say, and do,
That she can go on and pass that legacy on to her children, too.

And one day we will be reunited in that great reunion in the sky,
That awaits all those believers who in Christ die.
And forever we will remain partners, buddies and close friends,
In the place where our joy and satisfaction never fades or ends.

T W O

In Pursuit of Freedom

I have come to discover in my walk with God, that freedom is not a single destination, but rather a journey along the way. In my pursuit, I found that freedom was not an outward attainment of some goal, but true freedom was the work God needed to do in me. My prayer is that through the poems inscribed on the pages to follow, you too will discover the freedom God desires to bring to you. God's purpose for bringing freedom in our lives is so that we can relate to Him on a more personal and intimate level. You may find the road to freedom involves pain from time to time as the Lord does His work of purging us of old mindsets, hang-ups, and ways we've always coped because of how we've been conditioned. But I guarantee you, the pain cannot compare to the gain! In many cases, the biggest obstacle on the journey towards freedom is ourselves, because we've allowed the effects of negative experiences from the past to shape our thoughts, attitudes, and outlook on life which oftentimes falls far short of how God intended us to live. Jesus came to set us free from the effects of the past so that we can move towards our destiny and experience the awesome plan He has for our lives. And so I invite you to join me on this journey of freedom. Though it may involve some pain as God completes His work in us and shapes us into His image, don't give up or faint in the process. Remember, it is a journey, so keep it movin'! I encourage you as you pursue your own journey of freedom, fight for it, stand in it, but most importantly, **walk** in your freedom…for He whom the Son sets free is free indeed! *(John 8:36)*.

Today is your day…TO LET FREEDOM RING!!

Letrice Weaver

My Soul Is Satisfied

"Oh but, Lord, let me try,"
One day I said to Him.
And so I tried to fill my void
With things that grew very dim.

Not knowing He was the only one
Who knew my every need.
For He made me with His hands
And He could set me free.

I said, "Oh Lord, be my guide,
My comforter and friend.
No one else can give me joy
Like You alone can rend."

He said, "My child, I've been waiting
To come and abide with you.
I love you like no other can
And I'll make your life brand new."

Now I don't have to worry
How to find sweet rest for my soul,
Because I've given up my burdens
In exchange for a lighter load.

He Is the Potter

At times I find myself wondering
If I'll ever know God's will.
Though I often get impatient
He reminds me to just stand still.

"I am the Potter," He often says,
"And your life is in My hands.
I know you can't see everything,
But what you can't, I can.

I am the true and faithful God
Who comes right on time.
And just when you get weak and tired,
That's the time I shine."

I am indeed in His hands
As He shapes my life each day.
My trust shall be in the living God
For He is the Potter and I am the clay.

When You Free Me From Me

When You free me from me,
You cause me to see possibilities.
Things that were unattainable before
Because my eyes were not on You, but on me.
When You free me from me,
You free me from the pressure of feeling guilty
Because through my weakness,
Your strength is perfected in me.
When You free me from me,
You free me from the spirit of inadequacy.
When You free me from me,
You expose the lies I've always believed.
When You free me from me,
Truth enters in and I am made free.
When You free me from me,
I am able to freely give
Because now I know
It's in You I move and live.
I no longer shrink back
Because I fear I'll be rejected;
I open myself up
Because I've already been accepted.
I no longer operate
Based on how I think or feel.
I now trust in the God who says,
"Just stand and be still."
When You free me from me,
I no longer try to impress
Because You've become the one
In whom my soul can now rest.
When You free me from me,
You set me on an entire new course.
You give my life a new direction

And I can go forward, because You are my source.
When You free me from me,
Fear must be cast aside.
It no longer remains my constant friend,
For it's now in You that I abide.

I realize the biggest god of all
That must be severed today,
Is the one I've always loved and adored
And the one I've always obeyed.

It's ME! It's ME! O Lord of Lords
I'm asking You to free.
I realize it's only through self-surrender
That I can walk in victory!
Oh what freedom I now feel
Now that self has gone.
I've entered the selfless realm
And my life is no longer the same.
It's not about me, O Lord,
Oh no, it's not about me.
You have freed me from myself
So YOUR glory may be seen.
When You free me from me,
I'M FREE! I'M FREE!
I'M FREE TO BE THE ME YOU'VE
CREATED ME TO BE!

I've Come to Realize

It's often through life's trials
When our eyes are filled with tears,
That we learn to totally depend
On the One who calms our fears.

So often we begin to think
We've gotten this far on our own.
We hadn't yet come to realize,
It's by His grace alone.

My testimony today is
That if you have great or small,
It all flows from the throne of God,
Who's King and Lord of all.

Don't put your trust in riches,
For they soon will fade away.
It's like the air that we breathe:
It passes day by day.

Put your trust in the One
Who says, "I'm God and I change not."
He's the one our hearts should trust,
Whatever our situation, whatever our lot.

I'm coming to the point in my walk
Where I must trust His sovereign hand,
Where I can say with all my heart
On Christ, the solid rock I stand.

I've finally come to realize
My life is not my own.
I must let go and let Him lead,
For He's God and God alone!

Through the Fire

He chose to take me through the fire,
Though I would've chosen another way.
I didn't understand the plan of God
Nor did I understand His delay.

Why couldn't He quickly deliver me?
And why was the fire so intense?
God said He'd be with me,
But His presence I couldn't sense.

After the many days of complaints,
Of wondering, "Lord, why me?"
Somehow I felt God speaking softly,
"Just trust my sovereignty."

"I am the God who sees it all
And yes, I'm in control
Though you may not know it now,
I have a plan that will unfold."

It's in the times of suffering
Where our faith is put to the test,
That we learn to trust that God
Will work things out for the best.

It's in the "furnaces" of life
Where all has gone haywire,
That God wants us to remember
He's with us through the fire.

Unless You Breathe

It's only when You breathed
That man became a loving soul,
So that he could commune with You
And make Your presence his abode.

It's that kind of breath I need
To sustain me day by day,
To hold me up in trying times;
Breathe on me I pray.

I need Your loving grace
To abound and flow my way,
To pick me up and strengthen me;
Breathe on me I pray.

Lord, I need Your anointing
To rest on me each day.
Without You I have no life,
So breathe on me I pray.

When things are running hectic
And it seems I've lost my way,
Let me stop and ask if You
Can breathe on me today.

It's only when I'm in Your presence
That You cause my eyes to see,
That You alone can breathe new life;
So Lord, breathe on me.

The Secret Place

In my secret place, I'll renew your strength.
I'll refresh you. I'll restore you.
I'll revive. I'll quench your thirst.
Drink of Me in the secret place.
There's living water in the secret place.

No worries are in the secret place.
No cares are in the secret place.
For they've all been left at the door.
My peace is present here…

Enter in now to the Holy of Holies and worship Me,
For this is where I pour out of my Spirit
Into the hearts of man.
This is where I tell you that you can do
Beyond what you think you can do.
It's in my presence where your faith is ignited
And higher in Me is where you've been invited.
So don't shrink back from wanting more of Me,
For it's only here that you're able to fully see
That I'm the God who brings refreshing winds.
And in times where you want to give up,
I'll be with you until the end.

My glory, my glory is what I want to reveal
In the lives of those who will fully yield
To my plan, my purposes and my ways.
My glory's revealed in those that obey.

I walk with those who walk with Me.
I talk with those who talk with Me.
I open doors you can't even see,
For I see things that are yet to be.
Let Me take you to higher heights
And places you've never been before.
Though it's unknown and unfamiliar,
I know the plans I have for you.

So come into my secret place
And find life forevermore.
It's when you seek Me with all your heart
That I'll renew you, refresh you, and restore.

It's in the secret place.
It's in the secret place.

Freedom

Free me from every restriction,
Free me from every chain,
Free me from every evil thought,
So that I may praise Your name.

Freedom is what I desire.
Freedom is calling my name.
Freedom is what I am after.
I have nothing to lose, but all to gain.

I am going for the prize, O God.
The prize You've set for me.
I say I can do all things through You,
For You've given me all I need.

I speak wholeness to my mind today
And I say you are made whole.
I have the mind of Christ in me
So doubt, confusion, and fear must go.

You shall no longer dictate to me.
You shall no longer rule,
For peace has taken residence here
And my limits have been removed.

Wholeness for my spirit and soul,
He doesn't do anything incomplete.
For my body's been made whole, too,
Now for the Master's use, I am meet.

God came to make His people whole,
He came to set us free
And just as He told Peter that day,
"Go and bring someone else from their captivity.

Go in the name of my Son,
For there is power in that name.
Go boldly and proclaim my victory
Over every hurt, sin, and shame.

Boldness my children is what you need
To carry out my work and plan.
Great grace I give to you this day
As you go in and possess the land.

Not by power, nor by might
Is what I say to you,
But trust my Spirit to lead and guide
In everything I've called you to do.

Feast upon my word dear ones
And your mind will be renewed.
Step into the realm of my Spirit
And transformation will take place in you.

I love you, my children,
For I have chosen and called you by name.
The pain of the past has been erased
And I give you double for your shame."

Victory, Victory is what I hear the Father say.
Walk in it, Walk in it, Walk in it today!
No more bondage, no more shame.
Freedom, Freedom is what I give to you today.

My Daddy Loves Me, He Is All My Delight

My Daddy loves me.
He makes my life complete.
He satisfies like no other can.
He gives me everything I need.
This void within caused me to search
For the completeness only He could provide.
I thought my spouse, money, or the ministry was it,
But I found it was only in Him I could truly abide.
For everything I needed really was in Him,
I had heard it said, but never really experienced it.
It was in the times I spent alone with Him,
That my need for security was filled to the brim.
He taught me the only way I could have joy
And experience its fullness and not just a part,
Was that I had to let myself go
And trust Him with my whole heart.
He told me He was not like any other
Because humans can hurt and disappoint.
But if I would open up my heart to Him,
He would heal and restore every broken joint.
It's taken many years for God to do His work,
Cutting through walls of hurt, pain, rejection, and distrust.
But I thank God for sticking with me,
'Cause sometimes the road got a little rough.
I didn't want to face those hurts from the past.
How could He not know how much pain they caused me?
But until I was able to give those things to Him,
I would never really know what it was like to be free.
You see those things had shaped who I had become.
They covered up the person God created me to be.
They kept me from experiencing "life to the full."
For real love, real peace, and real joy was far from me.
But now that I've come to know

This love I've always wanted,
Nothing can separate me now,
Not even the enemy's lies that have always taunted.

The Lord has removed the sting of rejection, hurt, and fear.
He's healed the places of my heart I once held so dear.
Now I am satisfied,
For He's made my life complete.
I stand in need of nothing now
'Cause my Daddy loves me!

For Such A Time As This

"To everything there is a season"
And I believe my time is here,
To go forth and do those "greater works"
Despite the obstacles, despite the fear.

Due season has finally come to me
And this season I cannot miss,
For God has been preparing me
For such a time as this!

Destiny

A place that I've always longed to be,
A place where dreams become reality.

A place of hope, a place of peace,
A place where my soul finds its relief.

A place I've never been before,
Uncharted waters and far from shore.

Yet I know it's in this place,
Where God releases His power and grace.

A place that I will surely attain
Because through Christ, I can do all things.

A place where God desires me to be,
A place I call my destiny.

Now That I've Gotten Up

Always wanting to hold on
Because I was afraid of letting go.
I had been selfish all my life,
So for me to give was a resounding no.

Always wanted to be in control,
Always had to know the plan.
I couldn't allow myself to be "out there"
With no way of knowing how to return to land.

Always tried to hold myself up,
To show that I was strong.
Didn't want anyone to know
I wasn't perfect, 'cause I thought that was wrong.

And so for years I hid behind
Someone I thought was me,
Never realizing I wasn't living at all
Because I had a false identity.

At times my fears would appear
And I'd try to push them aside.
But they were so strong and powerful,
They rose to the surface every time.

I thought I would never be free
From my fears and insecurities,
For all my life I believed the voice that said,
"This is how you'll always be."

Time after time I tried to break free
From the thoughts that plagued my mind.
I'd tell myself, "You _can_ do this,"
But that mindset within won every time.

Sometimes when I tried to step out,
I got excited because my foot was out the door.
I'd tell myself, "This is it.
I can't take it anymore!"

But slowly I began to feel
The limitations all over again.
I told myself this couldn't be happening
'Cause I was strong and had the power to win.

But there I was, defenseless
Against the enemy in my mind.
I had no power within myself
To defeat these thoughts of mine.

I would hear them so clearly
Every time I told myself, "I can!"
Just like water off a duck's back,
My words had no power to stand.

As I began to ask God to fill my mind
With thoughts that came from Him,
Something started happening on the inside;
I couldn't explain it, except I was changing within.

As I began to hear and study His word
And read about a new way to live,
It seemed like I was getting stronger.
I even started learning to give!

My selfishness started slowly giving way
As I saw others in need.
I found out it's more blessed to give
Than it is to receive.

I learned that I no longer had to fake it,
That it was okay "to let 'em see you sweat."
For in my weakness, God's strength was perfected,
And that was as good as it could get.

I no longer had to hide behind
The mask of who I thought myself to be
Because in His word,
I had found my true identity.

But there was still this battle
That continued to rage and rage.
My mind was the battleground for this fight
And Faith vs. Fear were the ones engaged.

I knew I was the deciding factor
On who would win or lose.
Would I continue to see my life
As "half-empty" or "half-full?"

My outlook had everything to do with it.
My perspective had to be changed.
Was I going to live the life Christ promised
Or settle for a defeated life in exchange?

He died that I might live again
And know His resurrection power.
So why would I waste the life Christ gave
And allow satan to cause me to shrink back and cower?

I had to make a decision
To leave the thoughts I once knew,
The thoughts that have controlled me all my life
And had shaped my point of view.

I had to die to that old way.
I had to leave it behind,
For I knew Christ was calling me forward;
I had to cross the finish line.

I could no longer carry the old mind,
As familiar and close as it was to me.
I had to have it made over and renewed,
So that I could see my possibilities.

As I'm dying to the old me,
With all its limitations,
I am able to now experience the true meaning
Of my Emancipation Proclamation!

Christ came that I might have life
And have it more abundantly.
Because of His death and resurrection,
I have power over every fear and insecurity.

It is a New Day!
Let freedom ring loud and clear.
Christ has come to set at liberty
All of those who've been bound for years.

And now that I can get up,
I'm leaving this old place.
I'm being renewed in the spirit of my mind
And my thoughts are being reshaped.

I'm changing the source of my thoughts.
I'm no longer thinking the same.
The victory had to be won in my mind.
Now God's word is what I claim.

I give all the glory to God,
For His word now lives within.
My journey has only just begun
Because He has taught me how to win.

No more small and limited thinking
That caused me to see a half-empty cup.
My mind's been changed, my vision renewed,
Now, that I've gotten up!

And now, God says to you…

"Get up! Get up! Get up my child,
For the fog that has blinded you is gone.
I have freed you from the enemy's power.
Get up! For <u>your</u> new day has dawned!"

I Am a Queen

I am a Queen.
My Father gave me that name.
I am a Queen
And I'm no longer ashamed.
I am a Queen.
That's who You made me to be.
I leave my past behind.
I no longer allow it to define me.
I give You my hurt.
I give You my pain.
I give You my heart
And I ask You to reign.
For You alone know
The struggles I've had to face
And why it can be so hard
To accept Your royal embrace.
But I choose today to open my heart
And give You what I've held inside.
The shame, the hurt, the inner turmoil,
The anger, the rejection, and all I've tried to hide.
Cleanse me, Lord,
Through and through.
Heal me, Lord,
And make me new.
Today I make the declaration,
In spite of all my past regrets.
Because You make all things new,
"The world ain't seen nothin' yet!"
God turned what the devil meant
For evil into something great.
My life is now a testimony
Of God's love, mercy, and grace.
The journey's been rough.

The road's been long,
But God has turned my mourning
Into a dance and a song.
I know it is only
Because of Him, I am here.

That's why I'm so grateful
He took the time to draw me near.
He brought me into a deep, abiding love,
A love that no other can ever provide.
His love has healed me and made me whole
In places where the enemy had set up his strongholds.
But now that God
Has done a work in me,
I can tell others
Of how He's given me victory.
I am a Queen.
Did you hear what I said?
My past is gone, buried, it's dead.
The glory of the Lord
Shines forth through me,
For it's His beauty
He wants the world to see.
I am a Queen.
There's a crown on my head.
I am a Queen,
No longer looking back, but I'm looking ahead.
I am a Queen.
My Father gave me that name.
I am a Queen
And I'm no longer ashamed.

Forward

No more anger, My dear, I have taken your pain and strife.
My desire has always been for you to live a purpose-driven life.
No more being defeated – I've done away with that mentality.
For now that I am in your life, you have a NEW personality.
Your path has been mapped out and I have ordered your steps.
I also stood by your side with each and every tear that you wept.
You were never alone; I always promised I would be there.
The good and bad times, My child, together we did share.
The road has seemed rough, this life hard at times, I know,
But each trial and tribulation was purposed for you to grow.
To grow into the person that I have called you to be,
To live a life that is holy and pure – to live that life victoriously.
So, My child, stop and look – see how far you have come.
Look at that old lifestyle and see what I delivered you from.
I have thrown away the old and today you are brand new
And I have also placed My Spirit on the inside of you.
So go now, My child, for you have been prepared
To deliver and set free those who the enemy has ensnared.
So step out and move forward, you are My chosen one,
And in you I am well pleased and from My heart I say well done!

The Invitation

When your heart is heavy, come talk to Me…
I'll open your eyes so you can see.
There is power and victory in My Name.
Bring Me your burdens, guilt and shame.
Let Me cleanse your heart and your mind I'll renew.
I died on the cross so I could do this all for you.
Your life is so important to Me, more precious than the purest gold.
It is a part of the greatest love story that ever will be told.
So come now, My child, rest in My arms or sit at My feet.

Just give it all over to Me and let Me make you complete.
No more searching this world for pleasures that won't last,
No more feeling condemned by the guilt of your past.
Let it all go, My child, and give it to Me.
So I can make you whole, complete, and free!

<u>It is finished</u>

I shall have the victory, just you wait and see,
For my Lord has already spoken a promise of dominion to me.
Don't get this twisted; this isn't another puffed up front.
I'm serious about this now and to see you defeated is what I want.
No longer will you wreak havoc in the lives of the ones I hold dear.
No longer will you cause there to be bondage; no longer will you cause
there to be fear.
No longer will you lie, using games of trickery and deceit.
No longer will you cause others to wallow in self-defeat.
Take this as your notice; it's time for you and your imps to flee.

In the Name of my Savior Jesus and by His authority,
Victory is Mine for His word is 100% satisfaction guaranteed.
And I am standing until the end, and this time I will not concede.
My Lord has equipped me and I am ready for this fight.
For victory is mine by His Spirit, not strength or might.
My Lord has spoken and His word, it is true.
This fight is over and the loser is YOU!

T H R E E

Musings of an Earth's Sojourner

My Bible tells me I'm just passing through this world on my way to my intended home, Heaven. In this collection, I've shared some of my thoughts from different seasons along that journey. Much like Nikki Giovanni said in her poem, "Boxes," I also write because I have to. My pen is the gift God has given me to sort through my thoughts, prayers, tears, and dreams. I call my writing therapy, while others call it beautiful. This is why I share.

Ardener E. Lott

Growing

Sinner's Plea

written as a child concerning my salvation at age 12

65

Save me from this sea of sin,
This stormy sea of hate I'm in.

I know You died to save my soul,
I am the clay, and God my mold.

All my hope
And all my faith,
My strength to live
From day to day…

All these things I give to Thee,
Jesus, My Hope, please set me free.

WE GOT IT

written for students of the STAR Project
summer 1993

We got color and we got jazz.
We got soul and we got pizzazz.
We got power and we got might.
We like the dark, so later for light!

We don't just walk down the street, we strut.
To greet a brother, it's more than "what's up?"
You give him a slide, a snap, and a pound.
That's the only way ta be down.
'Cause down is where we all gotta git,
Down with our blackness, yeah, that's it.
There's no other way that I'd wanna be,
But blacker than blacker than black, you see.
'Cause black ain't a color you know, it's an essence,
The mark of God and His continued presence.

'Cause
We got color and we got jazz.
We got soul and we got pizzazz.
We got power and we got might.
We like the dark, so later for light!

We like music 'cause it's in our soul.
It's time to forget all the lies you've been told,
Like "black folks naturally have rhythm and speed!"
Discern what you hear versus what you believe.
In Africa, we used our drums to talk.
Some of those rhythms, we never forgot.
It's simple as that, no gimmicks nor theories.
Ancestral survivals, we see very clearly.

'Cause
We got color and we got jazz.
We got soul and we got pizzazz.
We got power and we got might.
We like the dark, so later for light!

So listen close as our story begins.
As we weave our web, we'll be drawing you in
Into a world full of poetry and color.
You won't wanna leave 'cause this world's like no other.
One that is dark with no room for bleachin'
So open your mind to entertainment and teachin'.
Come on inside, don't just stand at the door
And I'll tell you again like I told you before!

'Cause
We got color and we got jazz.
We got soul and we got pizzazz.
We got power and we got might.
We like the dark so later for light!

When Hanna Prayed She Said

"My heart rejoices in the Lord."

To think,
The Lord has brought me so, so far.
He's been my guide and shining star.

I turn my back and go my way, and think,
I don't need His help today.

He guides my feet and keeps me safe
While gently nudging in His loving way.

I stumble blindly on without a care,
With Satan nearby and quite aware.

The harmful demons God sends away,
Yet He permits a few weaker ones to stay.

You see, Satan only operates with God's permission
To strengthen His children or teach them a lesson.

So depression and sadness are hanging around.
Loneliness pitches in to bring me down.

But my God who is merciful, kindhearted, and great
Would never deliver an unbearable weight.

I realize my fault and with tears in my eyes,
I fall on my knees and look to the skies.

He waited with patience 'till I came around
To raise me up, He first brought me down.

My happiness, contentment, and joy are restored.
And I, too, can say, "My heart rejoices in the Lord!"

Christianity 101

October 2006

Depending on myself,
My abilities,
What I think I know,
What's logical,
Even my gifts,
Is a recipe for repeated disaster.

Looking to You
And depending on You,
Constantly seeking You
For direction,
For answers,
For guidance,
For everything,
Is my sure fire recipe for perpetual success,
So says Proverbs 3:5-6.

Learning

Browntown, U.S.A.

Written in East Liberty, PA
June 1992

I sit on my crate in the alley.
No one even notices me.
The sounds so sweet,
A cacophony of rhythms and images,
Noisily soothing me.

Old men with too big pants,
Shirts too small, smellin'
Of old cigars, laughin',
Smilin' those old black brother smiles,
Remindin' you of
Great Uncle Joe or grandpap.

Sisters gossipin' 'bout how
Nay-nay's havin' Bonay's child,
An' ain't even got no job!
An' Leshaun hit the number,
Got her baby some gold,
A Coach, an' some pumps,
But ain't paid light,
Phone,
Or gas bill the first!

Senior sisters with angelic,
Silver hair tucked behind soft ears,
Sweet-smellin', still dignified after
Centuries of holdin' our people together.
Mole-spattered faces holdin' bright,
Lovin' eyes fully sincere prayers
For you and yours,
Greetin' each other with "God bless yous"
And "How ya holdin' ups?"

71

Semi-fly older brothers,
Holdin' on ta when they useta be *it,*
Sportin' white or tan patent-leather shoes
In fall or winter,
At least one button un-done,
Glidin' 'cross the sidewalk,
Darin' you to think they ain't cool!

Babies totin' babies,
Swearin' they grown,
Child in one arm,
School books in another and
A monkey on her back so fierce
She can hardly hold her head up
To take the next step,
So busy searchin' for a daddy,
She forgets to be a mommy and
Can't figure why
"That child don't know how ta act!"

And in the midst of all that...
Breathtakingly beautiful,
Brown babies,
Stumblin' along behind someone's
Draggin' hand,
Oblivious to all the
Beauty and possibility
Of the culture that surrounds them
And is theirs to inherit.

Stuck on Strut

For God's Supermodels (S.E.S.)
May 2003

U Step sistah,
Step on…

Step on outta the negativity of your past, out of those lying lead boots the devil's got weighing u down and takin' the pep outta your step and tellin u u can't walk on cause u were…
Abused, raped, degraded, used, molested, manipulated, fired, adopted, mother 2 an aborted child, beaten, prostituted, forgotten, and downright mistreated. Now don't look shocked and don't be shushin' me 'cause there's no shame in a past which has God in its present, so u step! Step on outta those lead boots and tell the devil he better step, while u step on. Better yet, tip on and tell him u r still standin'. Like Antwone Fisher, but standin' on the promises that cannot fail. Promises that tell u that all that stuff doesn't matter 'cause you've been redeemed, bought with a price. Promises that tell u that all things (both good and bad) work together 4 good 4 those who r called according 2 His purpose! Now, don't get me shoutin' in here, I better stay on track…

U just step on, and stay!

U Stay sistah,
Stay on…

Stay on the right path, the straight and narrow, for narrow is the road which leads 2 life. So u stay. Stay on that treadmill, court, bike, or track even when u feel u can't go on. U stay on that job and be Esther, knowing that u r there 4 such a time as this, and u take that tired boss, that tired pay, and your tired co-workers, and u praise God 4 them and for the opportunity 2 shine your light in such a tired, dark place. U stay on those children and raise them, mold them, hold them, love them, correct them, encourage them, believe in them, and pray for 4 them and train them up in the way they should go, and when they are old…well, u know the rest, but y'all don't get me started, let me recap…

U just step on, stay on, and strive!

U Strive sistah,
Strive on…

Strive on and set your goals at such a lofty altitude that they can't be reached without the very hand of God in it. U press toward the mark for the prize of the high calling. Strive on 2 fan into a flame the gifts God has deposited in you. U strive on and strain to develop your teachin', your typin', your preachin', your planning, your writing, your witnessin', your modelin', your mothering, your singin', your servin', or whatever your gifts are. Don't u insult your creator by leavin' those gifts unopened, unused, or undeveloped. Now I know I was tryin' 2 make a point here…

U just step on, stay on, strive on, and sway!

U Sway sistah,
Sway on…

Sway on into the very presence of your God as u enter in and offer up your sacrifice of praise into your, Baptist, Holiness, Pentecostal, COGIC, AME or Nondenominational House of Zion, faith, praise, spirit, fellowship, worship, love or truth, under your bishop, doctor, pastor, elder, reverend, or brother so-and-so. Cause u know it's all just words which can't even begin 2 encapsulate the indescribable vastness, breadth, and depth of the love the one true God in Trinity has 4 us if we would but believe and receive it. But again, I digress…

U just step on, stay on, strive on, sway on, and shine!

U Shine sistah,
Shine on…

And this ain't no worldly, Hollywood kinda shine that'll wear off or burn out, it's here to stay! And u had the nerve 2 useta wish u looked like Naomi Campbell, Janet Jackson, Jayne Kennedy, Dianne Carol, or Lena Horne. Chile, don't u know u were created in the very image of Almighty God and those sistahs wish they had a piece of what u got goin' on?!?! This ain't the "high pro glow" y'all but the "u oughta know." Yeah, u oughta know my Jesus for yourself and then He can shine in u illuminating all the bleak, dim places and people in your life 'til your shine is the kinda contagious that people are linin' up 2 get a taste of. Now, I'm tryin' 2 get somewhere here, so as I was saying…

U just step on, stay on, strive on, sway on, shine on, and strut!

Yes, U Strut sistah,
Strut on…

Strut on and hold your head high and don't miss a beat and don't look down and don't look back cause the best is yet to come and the future is brighter than the blazing equatorial sun shining down on the queens of Africa surveying the beauty of their land sculpted by their God and reflective of their inner glow emanating to bathe and warm their black, brown, chocolate, coffee, caramel, tan and cream babies born to live, grow, love God and strut on like their mamas struttin' on this day with God in their hearts 'cause the spotlight is on and it's time 2 shout, "He's brought me from a mighty long way!" So, my sister, I'm finally done, I made it to strut so I'm gonna stop and sit, and smile as u…

Step on, stay on, strive on, sway on, shine on, and STRUT!

Imani Winds

October 2003

Imani Winds…
Winds of change rustling rapidly through music's history,
Blowing the dust off the pages of the chamber music chapter
Writing anew, in fact its final pages.

Wind is colorless, invisible most would say,
But not these winds.
They're colored rich cocoa, sweet caramel, and savory (with and without the cream).
They're visible, tangible, tasteable even…
Kinda like crossin' figgy pudding and mama's banana pudding.
Not a usual combo, and yet u can't get enough.

Imani Winds…
Extraordinary winds,
Winds dancing upon my heart strings,
Taking me to a place far away from dishes and diapers and my life's drama.

I could close my eyes and absorb the nuances of the notes as they rise up
2 meet me in the balcony.
But then I'd miss half the fun,
The fun of watching the winds as they blow, and blow and blow me a flirtatious kiss.
Drawing me into the party,
As they bop, lean, smile, glance & make me wish I was in on the secret.

Imani Winds…
Awe inspiring winds,
Winds strong enough to pull children
From the ghettos of our nation to the stages of our world.

Teaching, reaching, preaching, without a word
Painting bold, beautiful, breathtaking splashes of color
On a dusty, old white canvas
Giving it life, making it art, blowing us away, while we don't mind the trip.

Imani Winds…
Faithful Winds,
Winds faithful to your vision, your God, your people, your craft…

Thank you for sharing your gifts with us,
For bringing God glory as u blow on, and up,
And beyond…
Even your highest aspirations.

Living

Easter Sunday in Washington, D.C.

The chaotic harmony of a capitol
Teaming with anticipation of spring,
Marked by delicate cherry blossoms
And a collage of colored faces.

The twinkle of laughter
From chocolate-bunnied lips,
Blending sticky kisses
With cheeks of their chocolate mamas.

Bedecked as melons, emeralds,
Tangerines, sapphires and limes
Royalty, children of the King!

Puttin' it on for their Jesus,
Their Rock,
Their Sword,
Their Shield!

On monument lawns,
In hot storefronts,
Or under
Newly constructed roofs
Of million dollar,
Full city block,
Smorgasborgs of praise,
With voices lifted
In hallelujahs
And holy shouts
Of joy, adoring
The Risen Savior!

The Measure of a Man

April 2002

The measure of a man
(contrary to popular belief)
Isn't in his paycheck,
But it's in his determination.
Does he duck and run at the first sign of trouble
Or does he meet trials head on, with God as his guide?

The measure of a man
Isn't in his biceps,
But it's in the power of his prayer.
Does he fall prey to satan's schemes
Or does he put demons to flight when he falls to his knees?

The measure of a man
Isn't in what's parked in his driveway,
But what's in the depths of his heart.
Does he seek to make more money, to conquer and to win
Or does he focus his attention on God's plan and on His will?

The measure of a man
Isn't in the size of his black book,
But the only thing that matters is if he's in the Book of Life.
Does he struggle with solving his own problems
Or has he surrendered all to Christ the solid rock?

So whether single or married,
Father or friend,
Ahead or behind,
Worth a billion or a buck...

When measuring a man,
Don't fall victim to the hype.
'Cause if he lines up with God's Word,
Then for sure, he measures up right.

I NEED YOU

*Inspired by a message from Pastor Sabrina Mangrum
To the W.O.R.D Women on May 12, 2007*

I need You to teach me
What You want me to know.
I need You to stretch me
So that I can grow.

I need You to change me,
Day by day,
To do a new work.
Help me walk a new way.

I need You to form me
Into the new me,
Ready and able
To bear fruit for thee.

I need You to create me
New and afresh,
To mold a new me
Who can pass any test.

I need You to know me
Intimately.
Make my thoughts and ways
Mirror Thee.

I need You to rule me,
For I can't handle it all.
I know if I try,
Pride will precede my fall.

I need You to crush
My desires and my will.
Give me such an urgency
That I can't sit still.

I need You to throw me
Into the fire.
I need You to reassure me
You'll be there all the while.

I need You to launch me
Into the battle
And prep me for the race,
Like a jockey in the saddle.

I need You to heal
My spiritual infirmities.
When old patterns arise,
Help me fall to my knees.

I need You to forgive me
And restore me to You,
That my ways will be pleasing
And my thoughts will be too.

I need You to show me
My way of escape
When sin comes a-knocking,
May I turn down my plate.

I need You to spare me
From laxity of the spirit.
If I begin to stray,
Convict me so I feel it.

I need You to cleanse me
That my heart can be pure,
Then renew my spirit
That my steps may be sure.

I need You to banish
Fear and doubt from my mind,
To convince me I can
As the strongman You bind.

Finally, I need You to watch
As I make You proud,
As I move in Your power,
No longer fearing the crowd.

I need You to show me
Which path to follow.
On my mark,
Get ready,
Get set,
And now GO!

Mourning

For First Lady Brown

on the passing of Rev. Brown
December 8, 2003

Though your grief now is dark & heavy
And your load seems too much to bear,
May you find the strength you need
To cast on God every care,
To take it to the Lord in prayer.

While you now have a hole in your heart,
Once filled by the love of this man,
That old song says, "Jesus will fix it"
And I'm a living witness He can.

He may not fix it this instant,
This month, or even this year,
But His promises are checks you can cash,
Paid in full, so have no fear.

Our God is that balm in Gilead,
That faithful friend to hold near,
To comfort you as you grieve,
For the passing of someone so dear.

So shed your tears as you must
And give to Him all your fears,
For He's the one who can turn them
To blessed assurance the rest of your years.

As he served God here indeed,
We know he'll serve Him well up there.
Remember God's timing is perfect,
When your heart wants to cry, "It's not fair!"

Reverend Brown touched so many lives
And he'll want us to do the same.
If we live our lives spreadin' the Gospel,
Then his won't have been lived in vain.

May you savor every memory.
May you keep his legacy alive.
As you guide the grands and greats,
Keep your eyes on the eternal prize.

Remember he's not lost forever.
He's just present with the Lord.
Weary of battlin' earth's demons,
He can at last lay down his sword.

Can't you just see him dancin' in heaven,
Strollin' those streets of gold,
Singing God's praises forever,
With a body that won't ever grow old?

But don't you think he's not watchin'
To see how you're carryin' on.
He's saying, "You just keep on for Jesus,
And don't you sit down too long.
For there's much too much work in the vineyard,
For you to keep singing sad songs.

So keep working while it's yet day,
For the Master will not tarry long.
Keep your lamps trimmed and bright,
For the Master will not tarry long.
And don't you feel no ways tired,
For the Master will not tarry long."

Mourning

For my siblings
January 2006

I mourned the life of my dad today,
Yet I could not mourn that he'd passed away.
I mourned instead the life he lost while still living,
The stuff that he missed, things I should have forgiven.

He missed my senior year, my MVP's.
He missed my little sister's spelling bees.
He missed tears of joy and cries of pain,
Missed all the sunshine and the rain.

Missed the trips and the milestones one by one,
But most of all he missed the sheer fun
Of seeing his children grow day by day,
Without the invitation, will, or guts to stay.

His riotous living caught up in the end.
The brain struck a blow the body couldn't mend.
So he floundered and struggled to make sense of his words,
All the while looking and sounding absurd,
Especially to those who knew & loved him well,
And saw that the stroke had left only a shell
Of the man who could win a crowd with his smile
And then open his mouth and completely beguile.

It's laughable that with all of the crap that he dealt me,
I somehow was able to love him completely.
To look past indecency, absence and falsehood,
And weep for a soul that was misunderstood.

So I thank God for the breaking of cycles and for choices,
For gifting us poets with therapy called voices,
To speak of truth, lies, love, hurt and core feelings,
To allow us to share then move forth toward our healing.

FOR AUDE

July 2007

As I sit in this hospital room,
I wonder if you're there.
I watch the nurses come and go,
Not knowing if they care…

That you're my mom and I've got just one,
And it's hard to see you go.
Remembering how you used to say,
"Some folks have a hard row to hoe."

Your row may have been hard, an uphill climb,
But you took it all in stride.
Sustaining life with strength and grace,
With the Lord your God by your side.

So I rest assured of one great thing,
That your name's in the Book of Life.
And that if you go, it'll put an end
To this world's dose of grief and strife.

For you've fought the good fight and run your race,
And earned a few crowns I'm sure.
And I pray the riches you missed here on earth,
Await you at Heaven's door.

Where you'll see your mom and I pray a few more,
That you bade farewell on this side.
Where you'll dance and sing and praise the King,
Forever with Him you'll abide!

As I picture you there, my heart's suddenly aware
That that's just where I'd like you to be.
At home with the Lord; perfect peace, one accord,
Joyful, eternally!

Loving

NEWSFLASH

For Fred & other good black men
June 1996

Hey "Mr. Smug" on the evening news,
You say black men are robbers, killer and thugs,
Who prey on their own, wearing grins on their mugs.
I smile to myself as I say you a prayer.
You ain't seen mine...you just ain't seen mine.

Where have you been?
Haven't you heard?
There's a new breed of brothers who feed on God's Word!

Hey "Mrs. Researcher" in your clinical lab,
You think black men and fatherhood just do not fit,
They're irresponsible and afraid to commit.
I laugh in amazement and utter a prayer.
You ain't seen mine...you just ain't seen mine.

Haven't you heard?
Where have you been?
There's a new breed of brothers who are family men!

"Mr. Guidance Counselor" with your preconceived notions,
You say Uncle Sam's lookin' for a few black men.
Higher education just isn't the thing for them.
I look at my man and say a prayer of thanksgiving.
You ain't seen mine...you just ain't seen mine!

Haven't you heard?
Aren't you down?
This new breed of brothers is academia bound!

To my misguided sisters who've given up hope,
You say they're all gay, in jail, or no good,
You'd even spell "man" D-O-G if you could.
For you I shed tears, 'cause I've been there before.
Stop settlin' for mess! Keep your faith in the Lord!

I mean, where have you been?
Haven't you heard?
There's a new breed of brothers who live by God's Word!

Girls I know mine is fine, but he's officially off the market.
But don't be discouraged by my song of praise,
'Cause I don't mean to imply mine's the only good man left...
But I am saying, quite simply, that he is the best!

Vanessaness

For "Rev. Swan"

Before your conception...

'Twas an empty space in the world that only you could fill,
So God designed a "one-in-eternity" creation...
And called her **Vanessa**.
Never before was there one like you
And never again will there be another.
It's your "Vanessaness" that makes you so unique.

What on earth is "Vanessaness"? I can hear you asking.
Well, it's kinda like you saying, "Christian, no lie."
Only those who are blessed to see and love the real you,
All of you, can understand.

Vanessaness is the preacher
Who inspires us to a new level of obedience
Even if we have to "do it afraid."

Vanessaness is the wife
Who inspires us to assume the posture of a servant,
Joyfully attending to our spouses' faintest need.

Vanessaness is the hostess extraordinaire
Who inspires us to make our homes a warm refuge,
Where folks can find rest and peace for their weary souls.

Vanessaness is the Afrocentrist
Who wears her crown of locs
Naturally, regally, and inspires us
To see and remember
The forgotten beauty of our people.

Vanessaness is the mother
Who inspires us to prayerfully study our children,
So we can love them personally
And not be too proud to listen
When God uses them to teach us a lesson.

Vanessaness is the prophetess
Who inspires us to walk in our gifts
With holy boldness,
Not fearing the devil's whispering lies.

And all that's just a glimpse of Vanessaness,
'Cause God's got so much more in store.
And we'll be waiting, praying,
And anticipating with you
All the great things that God is ***still*** gonna do
To finish creating the Vanessaness of you!

A Letter to My Hero

For Fred

Hello Baby,

It's me again. I just need a moment of your time.
I know it's been a while, but something in my spirit told me
That I needed to reach out and touch you.

You know, touch you in that certain spot,
In that certain way,
That takes you to that certain place
Where your toes curl and you feel you are the king of the world.

To stroke your...
Do I have to say it out loud
To spell it out for you?
Come on, you know, to stroke that man's thing...
Your E-G-O!

Have I told you lately that you are the man of my dreams?
That if there were a man-makin' machine,
And I could punch in my
Needs
Desires
Preferences
Fantasies
That it would spit me out a carbon copy of you?

Have I told you lately
That you are my security blanket?
That your
Love
Protection
Provision
Care
Allow me to rest easy,
To be anxious about nothing, just knowing you are there?

Have I told you lately
That sometimes when I'm
At work
In my car
At the mall
A suspicious little smile sneaks across my face
And causes passersby to wonder what I have that they don't?
I wanna tell them that it's you!

Have I told you lately
What a blessing it is to know
That our children don't have to look outside our home
For a good role model?
Not a perfect one,
But one who seeks to model Christ
And is man enough to say,
"I'm sorry,
I was wrong,
Daddy made a mistake?"

Well, if I haven't told you,
I'm telling you now.
For they say the measure of a man
Can be read in his wife's eyes.
Well I know my eyes are smiling,
Because they're looking at you,
As you're looking at Him.

Love Always,

Your Wife

Oh, and by the way,
Just in case you were still wondering,
You *are* the king of _my_ world!

INTRODUCTION

For Josiah on his dedication day
July 2003

Look out world, here I come.
Prince Josiah, son of some-
Body who goes by the name of Fred,
Our peaceful ruler, a.k.a., my dad.

I'm destined for greatness, 'cause my dad does things right.
He's there for our family morning, noon, and night.
I can see my future even now.
I'll walk in God's power.
Dad'll show me how.

He'll hold my hand,
Help me when I fall.
I'll be a giant in his eyes,
Whether I'm seven or five feet tall.

He'll teach me that
It's okay to cry,
That I don't have to act
Like there's dust in my eye.

He'll show me,
That where I am weak, God is strong.
That to boast in my limited strength
Is all wrong.

Since *he* has learned that,
He can now teach me.
He's breaking the cycles
In our family tree.

So…

Look out world, here I come.
Prince Josiah, son of some-
Body who goes by the name of Fred,
Our peaceful ruler, a.k.a., my dad.

You see that sparkle in my mom's eye?
Well God put it there by using her guy,
Her protector, her king, her covering, and ours too.
So my sisters and I will know what to do
When we stand before God and speak our vows,
Our spouses will know that we've been shown how
To live our lives with God as the center.
For this is the secret to a marriage that's a winner,
For a cord of three strands is not easily broken.
Back in 1997, no truer words were spoken.

So…

Look out world, here I come.
Prince Josiah, son of some-
Body who goes by the name of Fred,
Our peaceful ruler, a.k.a., my dad.

I'm here 'cause Dad came boldly to God's throne
Crying out for a man-child to call his own.
God answered his spiritual cry
In the physical realm.
My very life's a reminder
That God's at the helm,
That He doesn't need our calculating, assistance, or help.
He is simply God all by Himself.

He can take a child one day
And in weeks give another,
Bringing swift complete healing,
With no need to recover.
And to think, a God that BAD made me.
He thought a thought, spoke a word,
And I came to be.

So each time you see me,
Stop and give God His praise.
Pray I'll serve only Him
For the rest of my days.
If you do that for me, as my family,
Then I can boldly say…

Look out world, here I come.
Prince Josiah, son of some-
Body who goes by the name of Fred,
Our peaceful ruler, a.k.a., my dad.

Unsung Heroes

For Herbert Jefferson and other real black men
June 1998

I was searchin' thru volumes of praises sung by black poets,
Lookin' for a poem to dedicate to you.

I was stumblin' upon page after page of adulation and reverence,
For moms and grandmoms, when a thought suddenly hit me
And I asked myself, "Why is it our black mothers seem to receive ALL
the praise?"

Then I got a vision of some overworked, underpaid mama
With sweat on her brow, and hands on her ample hips,
Talkin' about, "Cause I don't see no daddy's carryin' y'all children around
for no nine months and then laborin' for nine hours to bring y'all here,
that's why!"

I thought to myself, "Yeah, right on sistah," but my soul still wasn't settled
and I thought and wondered on...

When our mama's feet were swollen from the weight of livin' and carryin' us,
I wonder who helped her prop 'em up and maybe even rubbed 'em a while.
And could her feet have withstood another day's journey
If our daddies weren't there?

And when our mamas found themselves unable to work for carryin' us and
worryin' about makin' ends meet,
I wonder whose hard work ethic and steady job eased her troubled mind.
And could her mind have focused on me, and sent me all those
Pleasant thoughts if our daddies weren't there?

And then the wonderin' started gettin' good to me,
So I wondered some more...

When our mamas got put on bed rest,
I wondered who made sure they were fed and did all those "mama"
Things that couldn't be done from in bed.
And could her rest have been a rejuvenatin', renewin' rest
If our daddies weren't there?

I wonder too...
When the doctor said our mamas shouldn't lift no heavy load,
I wonder who musta toted those groceries and rearranged that
Furniture, makin' space for me,
If our daddies weren't there.

I wonder...would I still be standin' here recitin' this poem...
Or would I be another miscarriage on somebody's list of statistics...
If my daddy wasn't there?

Well, I know I got this private school education
And I almost got a college degree that I know I wouldn't have
If my daddy wasn't there...

But it don't take all that learnin' nor no college degree
To figure out that all them black poets were wrong for not singin'
More praises to our daddies.

Well, I ain't no poet, and I can't sing you no song,
But since my daddy knows Jesus,
I know a little somethin' about praise.

And he taught me that Jesus wants everything that has breath
To praise the Lord.

Well, I'm takin' this time, and this day to praise the Lord for my Daddy,
And to tell Him that if no black poet ever gives Him thanks...
I am, and I will
On this day,
And every day for bein'

Not just a soldier, but a survivor,
Not just a provider, but a prayer,
Not just a fisher, but a finisher,
Not just an auditor, but an answerer,
Not just a warrior, but a worshiper.

Thank you, Daddy, for bein' our unsung hero.

Steal Away: A Christmas Poem

"Only seven days until Christmas,"
Josiah announces with a morning yell,
Interrupting my sleep,
Like a church tower bell!

"Shhhh," I request,
"Mommy's still waking up."
"Get up mommy," he squawks,
"Seven days won't be enough!"

"There's mountains of stuff
We still have to get done.
We need to get to the mall,
Gotta get on the run!"

"There are cards to address,
Christmas plays to be written,
Festive cookies to be made,
Cousin Kenna needs mittens!"

"Hold on," I tell him,
"Take a breath, slow down.
I just need some quiet,
Not a peep, not a sound!"

"Yes, mommy," he says
While perched on the bed,
While visions of I don't know what
Dance through his head!

"Where are your sisters?
Have devotions been done?
Is it even morning?
I don't see the sun!"

In romps, Dominique announces,
"Devotions done… hours ago.
Are you still in the bed?
Come on, let's go!"

"Let's go ice-skating,
It might snow, perhaps.
Mom, we've got no time
For your mid-morning naps."

Before I can answer,
Before I can speak,
Here comes Gabriella;
My chances look bleak

Of easing into the day,
Just my Bible and me.
Some sweet, sweet silence,
By chance some warm tea.

So I turn to the kids,
With a smile on my face,
Sweetly saying, "Get lost,
Give mommy some space."

Oh what a mean mommy,
What a cruel thing to say.
I know what you're thinking,
But it's okay.

It'll all become clear
As my rhyme unfolds,
How I can guiltlessly make
A statement so bold.

As their chattering quiets,
And they pad from my room,
I promise to rejoin them,
In due time,
Quite soon.

The door slowly closes,
I hear its soft click.
I slide to the floor,
Knowing I must be quick.

I rush to the prayer room,
Morning hair and stank breath.
He beckons, "Come as you are,
It's all good, I'm not pressed."

As I yield to His call,
Surrendering to His leading,
I steal away to my Jesus.
He's just what I was needing.

I spend time with Him there,
I bask in His presence.
Emerging changed,
My countenance is evidence

That I've been with The One
Who Christmas is all about.
He's changed my heart,
Cleared my vision, no doubt.

Before, all I could hear
Was the racket, their requests,
But after meeting with Jesus,
I remember, I'm so blessed.

To have 3 loud noisemakers,
Not one, count them, three!!
And a rambunctious husband,
Who is noisy as can be!

Though the days of the season
May be full of running and ripping,
As I steal away to Jesus,
I gain strength, I stop tripping!

So thank you God, for my family,
As loud and wild as they are.
They're also sweet
As can be.

So, I'll keep you no longer,
I'll close my short tale.
But before you go rushing
To one last sale,

I've got one little question,
One more thing to say.
Will you take time this season
To steal away?

F.H.G. December 2010

"Afterthought"

Curious, isn't it?! Why is an afterthought a bad thing? Reflection is always said to be a good thing: learning from words, actions (beneficial or detrimental). Then why do I feel so unimportant on our special day? Same old, same old. Familiar guilt, nothing new – to say or do. I guess you forgot about the afterthought.

"E-S-T-R-A-N-G-E-D"

E-s-t-r-a-n-g-e-d
Hmmm. Strange word.
With a range of meaning in application.
Relational...or at least, it used to be.
Now from him/her or even it, an old thing with a new adjective.
Implied trouble, tumult, tears. Once two, now one minus one. Maybe my math needs work,
But so do we...
Are you willing?

"Afraid of Me"

Afraid of what I don't know,
Terrified by what I do – "no!"
Is ignorance bliss?
What if what I don't know really can hurt me?
What then, my friend? Tell me.
If knowledge is power, then why don't I feel Empowered?
If knowledge is light and truth is right, then why don't I feel Enlightened?
And why does my dark-ness consume me...yet it's as if others can clearly see right through me.
No depth, no breadth, no substance, no value –
A shallow representation where the real deal should be.
Could be? May be. Can't be.
Perhaps, it's just fear that colors my vision,

That distorts the shape and size of my destiny,
That obscures the reflection I'd desire be,
And reduces my thoughts to lowest terms.
I must learn – to get it right, to see it right.
My future's bright and so am I.
My worth is not measured in letters and numbers,
But in how I use what I have to bless others.

"The Instrument I Am"

I am an instrument.
My lungs take in air, the wind necessary to blow across the cords of my
larynx with great precision.
Pitch, volume, and vibrato
I produce.
I am an instrument in and out of time, calculated cadence.
My heart palpitates with the rhythm of righteousness.
I am an instrument.
My hands, cymbals clapping, applauding, lauding, lifting, even splitting.
Truth and spirit yielding much
Offered to the Holy One.
Now and always, it's a must.
I'll give God all my worship.

"Sing for Me"

Lift your voice.
Let a sound be heard.
Sing for me, sing for me.

Pain has thrown me into discord,
No note resembling what it used to be.
Torment without a word.
Sing for me, sing for me.

Hurt so long I've forgotten, see,
How to properly make the melody.

Perverted notions, notations of fear,
Sulking, sinking de-bas-ing me.

Sing for me, sing for me.
Your voice sounds better.
Your life to the letter lives out loud
So all can see...and hear.
Oh dear, please sing for me.

Singing does not equal freedom
Nor does it indicate joy.

I thought I knew why the caged bird sang.
Maybe he danced, or buried his head in the sands,
As another sang the song he wanted to.

Sing for me, 'cause I can't anymore.
Where is the door?
I can't live a lie,
Standing behind my "why's".
No wis-dom ever attained...only PAIN.

And why should I sing?
Why should I announce the sting of the thing that keeps me silent?
No, better not inflict this pain on another, or taint the spirits of those
already afflicted
Like me, like me.
Naaw, it's better this way.
You sing, and I'll sit and let the silence cloak me.
Sing for me.

F O U R

Intruder in the Garden: Overcoming the Spirit of Rejection,
An excerpt from A Call to Intimacy – a Command to Answer

This chapter is from my book *A Call to Intimacy – A Command to Answer*. The chapter is my attempt to walk in the direction of my fears and express a few lessons taught by Pastor Peter Williams and Pastor Daniel T. Mangrum that challenged my prior experience and theology. The truth of this chapter is that what is not of faith is not of God and the place that I maintained in my heart for rejection was not a reflection of faith. It was, therefore, not of God and had to go. While it was not my desire to be rejected, the spirit of rejection lived within my heart because I made room for it to dwell, unchallenged and free to pollute my worship. Through this writing, I hope to encourage people to cast off any seeds of rejection that seek to live in their hearts, and to exercise their choice the next time the spirit of rejection seeks to make a home in the garden and forbid it entrance.

-Dianne Lesley Poole

They walked in the cool of the day. The foliage gave way to robust smells which made the imagination of Adam call this a rose and that a daffodil. The leaves voluntarily broke forth with

How did he get into the garden that day? Who did she think she was talking with and why did she talk with him as if they were old friends? How could he lead her down a path, which he knew would mean utter banishment from her home?

How? Because he was an intruder in the garden, and though she wasn't familiar with enemies and though his presence must have seemed odd, she was at home. Home is supposed to be safe; it's a place of refuge from those who could otherwise do you harm. It is a place where trusted friends gather. It's difficult to anticipate an enemy when you are in familiar settings or with familiar people. Hear King David's cry in Psalms 43:9, "Yea, mine own familiar friend, in whom I trusted, which did eat of my bread, hath lifted up his heel against me."

But Satan was no friend and he indeed meant Eve harm, and though the scripture reveals him as "the serpent," it was through him that we are introduced to a stronghold which has plagued the world from that day until this very second: the Spirit of Rejection. A few moments in Eve's home with the author of rejection caused God to do what He had no desire to do: evict His own creation from their home.

The Old Testament carefully narrates story after story of the sins of the father visiting the sons; Rejection moves down through the generations as if we had no hope.

Despite the apparent free roaming nature of the Spirit of Rejection, the truth is that we are not those who have no hope; rather, we are those who stand firm in Jesus. Recall how the axe has been laid at the root for many of the strongholds that we've already been delivered from; so it will be with rejection. Someone say Amen!

*Rejection, simply defined, is a negative
response to something sought after.*

Ask someone who walks in rejection or fears rejection and listen to their story as they talk about their fear of being refused or the memory of being denied. Soon to follow is the quiet comment or thought that they will never allow it to happen again.

Unconsciously they are saying that the hurt and disappointment, which resulted from the act of being rejected, has created a place in their heart that will never heal, and therefore to protect it they will never risk being rejected again. You or I may not make a conscious decision expressed that way, but I don't believe I am too far off.

Countless people resolve that it's ok that they've been hurt as long as it doesn't happen again, as if the prevention of an event and healing from a hurt are mutually exclusive. **If we decided to be one of those people who are content to hold onto our feelings of rejection and the wounds and scares caused by an act which resulted in our feeling rejected, there will be a consequence to our decision.**

That consequence being that you or I will be disqualified from intimate relationships in this area of the heart.

Feeling rejected usually stems from an act, something said or something done. It is also important to understand that we can encounter an act not intended to reject us, but the end result is still that we feel rejected. Also, despite how a rejection makes us feel alone, it does not operate in isolation.

Our Expectation + an Act Which Does Not Meet Our Expectation = an atmosphere where rejection can grow.

We must realize that what the above equation yields sometimes is determined by our expectation.

If we do not provide room in our expectation for people to fail, we are going to be disappointed. Disappointment is an emotion which expresses our dissatisfaction with the results of something or someone. Disappointment, left unchecked, will provide an open door for the spirit of rejection.

The posture of our hearts can also determine if the spirit of rejection makes a permanent or momentary stay. The Four Spiritual Laws track created by Campus Crusade for Christ, compares "The Self-directed life" with "The Christ-directed life" with the use of a throne encamped by the elements of our life. When Christ is on the throne of our hearts, there is order. However, the absence of Christ on the throne of our hearts means that self is postured on the throne, and there is confusion and the possibility of every work of darkness. It means that we are Open to the "wiles" of the enemy, including the spirit of rejection.

1. The Self-directed life.…..Self is on the throne. Interests are directed by self, resulting in discord and frustration. Christ is outside the person's life.

2. The Christ-directed life.…..Christ is on the throne. Self is yielding to Christ. Interests are directed by Christ, resulting in harmony with God's plan.

Understanding the process of Christ ruling the throne of our hearts is a lifelong walk. It's possible for us to have received Jesus as our personal Lord and Savior and at the same time maintain ruler-ship over certain areas of our life. It's always a good exercise to examine where "self" is ruling things in your life so that you can do as Paul declares to the Church at Corinth: "I bring myself under subjection, least after I have preached to others I might become a cast away."

Salvation is a decision made at a certain time, but the process of sanctification requires that we surrender our lives to the King daily. If you ever get a chance to hear Pastor Sabrina Mangrum[1] teach on the sanctification process, don't miss it. She has a clear revelation and helps us to understand that it's a process, one where one layer at a time must be removed.

While it is a process, it is also a choice. The Lord is ever ready to help us walk in the newness of life and to help us understand what His word declares to be true: that if any man be in Christ, he is a new creation. Old things are passed away; behold all things become new.

The "becoming new" process is something that we struggle with, and yet it's true and linked to the promised that "I can do all things in Christ who strengthens me." In light of that, I have a question:

---

[1] Cornerstone Peaceful Bible Baptist Church, Upper Marlboro Maryland.

Yes, you have a choice. Here I go quoting Paul again, but I must say that God's word has been a light in the pathway out of darkness, and it has certainly lead me down a road where the effects of rejection no longer have a hold on me. That said, Paul declares in Corinthians, "No temptation has taken you, except that which is common to man, but God is faithful and will not allow you to be tempted beyond that which you can bear."

When I joined Cornerstone Peaceful Bible Baptist Church in 1998, I was overwhelmed when I first heard Pastor Daniel T. Mangrum teach that I had a choice about being hurt. If I can do all things, then "all" must also mean I can bring my emotions under subjection and choose to believe God's word: that I am accepted in the beloved, thus rendering the spirit of rejection powerless in my life.

Rejection enters our lives unannounced, often deeply embedded in the heart of a friend, a trusted colleague, or even a family member. It is the residue to what is left behind when our expectations are not met. Rejection often begins with a desire in our own hearts. Please note it can be for something appropriate or inappropriate. Rejection can also come from desires deeply rooted in our hearts, which go undetected for years.

Over the years I have often wondered why the scripture says, "the heart is deceitfully wicked, who can know it," and yet it warns us to "guard the heart with all diligence for out of it proceeds the issues of life." James, the brother of Jesus, warns that it is the desires of the heart that cause a man to be tempted in one direction or another. James is so clear to say that the temptation to enter into sin is not because God is tempting us, but because of our desires which are in our own heart. Especially, those desire that we are aware of; which have lain dormant for a season, waiting for an opportunity to be fulfilled.

Let me explain that the Serpent didn't have anything to offer Eve. He, however, entered in looking to simulate her thoughts. Was it his intention for her to be banned? Was it his intention for her to experience rejection, due to her own sin? I can't say. What I can say is that the enemy was jealous of Eve's intimate relationship with God and he was interested in destroying that relationship. He wanted to draw her away from God and cause her to trust him and not God.

Note to self: the act of drawing you away from your Abba Father is an act which will compromise your intimate relationship with Him.

The account in Genesis reveals to me that the enemy's desire to have us worship him will be pursued at all cost and if he must manipulate us to lead us away from God, he will use rejection or any other intruder to accomplish his goal. A manipulator comes in and must operate in a spirit of deception if he's going to accomplish his goal. If that is true, nothing a manipulator does can be trusted. The enemy is a master manipulator. He comes in as if he is going to give us something that we strongly desire, something that we really need and oftentimes think we can't live without. And so we allow him in. There are times when we see a few warning signs, which come to warn us that something is not right. But the deep longing in us permits him to come in just this once, and the end result is worse than the beginning.

Please understand that rejection is a spirit, yet it will cause real physical pain in the heart of a man or woman. As I mentioned, rejection cannot work in our lives without a little help from us. Here's what I mean.

Some time ago, I had the opportunity to consider dating a young man. He was a lovely man: loved God, treated me with great care, extremely intellectual (which I must admit was the real drawing card), and loved to talk to me any time of the day. Over the course of time, I decided I didn't have any intention of marrying him, and so dating was out of the question. We decided not to talk with each other anymore. Well, over time I discovered that this gentleman was courting another woman while he was also occupying my time.

I later realized that despite the fact that I didn't want a relationship with him, I felt rejected. How could I feel rejected? It was an amazing discovery. Although I didn't want this particular gentleman in my life, I discovered that I did want someone to share my hopes and dreams with. I also had to admit to myself that I enjoyed having someone to call me and want my company. While I didn't solicit his company into the garden, I did welcome his presence once he came in. Despite the fact that I knew he couldn't stay in my life, I allowed him to linger. Why? Because his presence silenced my longings for companionship.

Now the dangerous thing is that I didn't even know that these longings were there. But indeed they were. I may have had things under control intellectually, but I certainly didn't have things under control emotionally, and that is where rejection targeted its attack.

Spiritually and intellectually, it was a no-brainer. However, after several days I began thinking about the fact that prior to me deciding I didn't want a relationship, he had chosen to have a relationship with someone else. And it was in the midst of that thought that rejection's seed was given room to grow...

As I was processing through this situation one day, I thought (too long) about how I missed conversation with this man, and my emotions began to stir. I thought (too many times) "he didn't want me!" At some point, the Holy Spirit shook me and I stopped in front of the bathroom mirror and said, "Shut-up Lesley Dianne!" Although I believe it was the enemy who wanted to plant the seed of rejection in my heart, it was "self" that was trying to open the door for the enemy.

It was time to bring those emotions under subjection, confess God's word, and cease speaking negativity over my own life. Let's be clear, his behavior was without cause and lacked integrity. I, on the other hand, had some responsibility.

What is my responsibility?

1. Speak Life
2. Agree with God about who I am
3. Speak Life again
4. Bring my "self" under the subjection of the Holy Spirit and God's word
5. Speak Life again
6. Guard my heart with all diligence, for out of it proceeds the issues of life.

There are times when the intruder enters into our lives without invitation or without any provoking from us. The scripture is clear: "he is roaming the earth seeking whom he may devour." But there are times when he enters because we have given way to him.

I know that there are those of you out there who are not experiencing intimate relationships with God, your husbands, wives, friends, or your children because you've been abused (this could be sexually, physically, emotionally, or verbally), abandoned and/or rejected, and the enemy is holding you hostage in the garden and feeding you lies about yourself. His lies are keeping you from walking freely and you think that the situation, which brought about your present condition, must have been your fault. If you are in, coming out of, or have been in an abusive situation, get some help and know that it is not your fault. This I know from experience.

For over 10 years of my childhood, I was being abused. The abuse ranged from physical abuse to emotional abuse. Whatever the abuse, it left me feeling as if I wasn't worth the price of dog food. I didn't feel loved, I didn't feel accepted, and I felt rejected, and growing up, every relationship would end with someone leaving me.

Understand that the person who abused me didn't walk away from me. But the abuse somehow communicated that I wasn't worthy of the love other young girls received, and because I wasn't worthy, I received this abusive type love.

As I got older I would seek men who would perpetuate the abuse as a means of feeling loved. I would later learn through my relationship with the Lord (and a good Christian counselor) that love is kind, and that true love *"gives at the expense of self for others."* This idea is contrary to what I understood as love: "takes at the expense of others to please 'self.'"

My home should have been a safe place, but it became the scene of a nightmare. My bed should have been a place which held my young virgin body, but it became a place of defilement. Whatever life was supposed to hold for me as a little girl had been rejected.

Once the abuse stopped, I put a guard at the gate of my heart. I vowed that no one would ever get to the once fertile soil of my heart. I lived a life where I rejected others before they could reject me. Although the abuse had ended, the feeling of rejection lived on in the deep crevasse of my heart.

Like an abandoned, blighted field there was a "do not enter" sign on my heart. But there was one who would dare enter-in.

God never debated how Satan got into the garden, and for that reason I spend very little time dwelling on those who hurt me. God's questions were to His children. Who told you? Knowing full well who told Eve. I believe God wanted to provide Eve and Adam the opportunity to confess their sin, to expose their weakness and not to lie. But they didn't, and a seed of rejection was planted that day.

I am not saying that God having to send Adam and Eve out of the garden was the source of rejection. I am saying that the manipulation of the enemy created a situation where Eve rejected the plan of God and where there was opportunity for a lie. Adam then joined her. The end result was banishment from their home and separation from God. It was in that separation that they met the spirit of rejection. We see it in their son Cain. Cain rejected the ways of the Lord for the way he wanted to do something. When presented with a choice as to how to worship the Living God, he chose another way. His decision to reject the plan of God made him think that God had rejected him. It was, however, Cain who first decided to do things his own way. This is important because it demonstrates that one can be impacted by the rejection as a result of choosing to walk according to the flesh. Think about King Saul. Indeed, God rejected him as King, but only after he rejected God's ways.

Don't be confused; you will have to make a decision for God or you will reject God. If you reject God's ways, don't conclude He has rejected you, but rather you have rejected Him.

Uprooting the Seeds of Rejection

When my father would get into a gardening mood, our Saturday was ruined. The work, though it looked simple, was never ending. My father was less interested in what the garden looked like from the window of my room, but was consumed with the condition of the soil in the garden. He wanted to plant greens, tomatoes and squash. I didn't mind pulling out the weeds, cutting the grass and planting a few seeds, but he wanted more. We were city girls and didn't always see the need for fresh vegetables. We spent hours digging up the dirt and turning it over, again and again. We then had to rake it and take all the foreign particles out. What was the point? It was just dirt. Finally, after hours of pulling weeds, digging in the dirt for roots (which were connected to stuff in our neighbor's garden) and then breaking up the fallow ground, it was time to plant the seeds. All that just to get something to grow. Why didn't he just go to the supermarket?

I must admit I was so short-sighted when I was little girl. However, two events have clarified this over the years: the first is a conversation I had with my mother that brought such revelation to me and the second is an experience I recently had at a Community Clean-up day in my neighborhood.

One Saturday evening, I was in the kitchen cooking dinner with my mother. She was asking me about everything and nothing. I assumed we were having general chatter, so I was running off at the mouth, which was my normal activity as a teenager. However well-orchestrated my mother's intent, I didn't see the object lesson coming in my direction. She asked about my day, and I explained: I cleaned the living room, cleaned the bathroom, read a few books, and played outside. She asked me what I did in the living room. I was baffled by the question, so I paused and asked what she meant. She wanted me to explain how I had cleaned up the living room, what first, and what second. After tripping over my words, because I now knew we were no longer having idle chatter, I just shut up and looked up at her.

Never turning from cutting the thigh from the body of the chicken and ensuring that the breast was cut ever so perfect (as this would be my father's piece) she said, "It appears you moved the furniture and put Old English furniture polish on everything. The living room smells good, and the new location of the furniture makes you think more has been done than it appears, but when I sat down I could see that dust was everywhere. Dianne, (she normally called me Les, I knew I was in trouble) you can't be afraid of hard work. To really clean the room you will have to spend some time looking under stuff and moving things, not shifting furniture to make it look like you did something. You have to clean under everything; you have to go looking for the dirt, and please don't put furniture polish on anything until you remove the dirt. Otherwise, it just attracts more dirt."

Just when I thought she was finished, she said "And for Pete's sake, don't be so lazy. Don't be afraid of a little hard work, it's always worth it in the end."

Lesson Learned: Cleaning of any space, even my heart, takes effort.

The second story occurred recently in my Ward Seven neighborhood in Washington, DC.

It was the second Saturday of September. My high school friend was visiting from Kansas City, the Community Clean-up was scheduled to start at 6:30 AM, I had another meeting at 8:00 AM, and our Women's Ministry meeting was scheduled at 10:00 AM. Igot up early to show my face at the Community Clean-up, then left so I could get to my meeting by 8:00 and our ministry meeting by 10:00. The challenge was that there were over 500 people at the Community Clean-up and most of them were not from my Community. I couldn't let it be said that 500 people came from around the city to plant trees in my neighborhood and all I did was show my face. I registered, got my t-shirt, and promised to be back a little later.

After all my meetings, I collected my friend from Kansas City, returned home, and rejoined the volunteers. Someone quickly handed me a shovel and pointed me to a few bushes which needed to be planted. "Dig up the dirt and plant them." That was my instruction. It's a good thing had a few instructions from my father tucked away in my memory banks. A dozen or so pushes of the shovel into the dirt, I realized that I needed to add a little elbow grease. I drove the shovel in the dirt one more time, took my right foot and planted it on the top of the shovel, and forced it deeper into the dirt. Finally, I thought we were making progress. After a few minutes, the dirt underneath the shovel pushed back on me.

Remember, although I didn't appreciate those Saturdays in the yard, I still learned a thing or two. I looked around and asked other workers if anyone had a pickaxe. The young lady to my right looked at me with an expression that said, "What are you talking about." At the same time, someone said, "Here you go, lady." You see, despite my wanting to lay in my room and read a book on those Saturdays, my father (both my biological and heavenly father) knew one day I would need to know how to work with dirt. I remembered my father's lecture: "You can break the dirt, put the shovel down and use something that can pierce through the dirt." I took the pickaxe, lifted it over my left shoulder, and with all my might I thrust it into the dirt. The first time the dirt was untouched by my hit, but I did it again and again, and on the third thrust the ground gave way. I could tell that the people around me thought I didn't know what I was doing, but they were wrong. I also knew that they thought the pickaxe wouldn't make that much of a difference. But I knew they were wrong. Being able to take the pickaxe, hoist it over my shoulder, and bring it back down was physics in motion. Thrusting is different than just pushing. The push would only be as strong as I was, but the thrusting would combine my power, with the force of the axe and energy or power gained as the axe went from over my shoulder to the ground. Look at what the dictionary says it means to thrust:

- To push or drive with force;
- To make a push; to attack with a pointed weapon;
- To push forward; to come with force; to press on; to intrude.
- A violent push or driving, as with a pointed weapon moved in the direction of its length, or with the hand or foot, or with any instrument; a stab;
- An attack; an assault.

The last thrust broke the dirt underneath my feet. In the middle of the dirt were huge roots, which looked like they had a million branches. The weight of that final hit caused a ripple effect across the entire patch of ground. It was crystal clear that something was growing underneath that hard ground. No one could see it from the surface, but it was still growing. No one was watering it, but it was still alive and no one knew who had planted it, but it was still there.

Lesson Learned:

If we hide the seed of rejection in our heart, it will grow and entangle itself in other areas of our lives. We have to go after rejection aggressively.

We can't embrace the emotions, sing songs that reinforce how wrong someone did me, engage in negative self-talk, or keep it a secret. It's best to tell someone how you feel and allow them to speak life. Don't invite people to commiserate the horror of being rejected. Find a friend who will sit with you, encourage you to see God's plan for allowing this into your life, and declare God's word, "all things work together for good" "if you establish yourself in the Word, God will order your steps." If these Scriptures are true then even the disappointment of not having our expectations met must work together for our good.

Lastly, allow God's love to bring healing, open up your heart, worship Him and let Him

"I'm Giving Them All to You"

God, I surrender my all to You.
The deepest areas in my life,
That only You can subdue.
I'm giving them to You, yes giving them all to You.
All the insecurities,
All the doubt inside of me,
The fear that's been controlling me,
I'm giving them all to You.
The thoughts that tell me to give in,
They tug and pull on my heart within,
And say to me, "You'll never win!"
But Lord I'm giving them all to You.
Everything You promised me,
That's what I now choose to believe.
No more bondage, OH God,
I choose to be free.

FIVE

Ballad, Beat, Blank Verse, Composition, Creation, Epic, Free Verse, Lyrical, Poesy, Ode to the Lover of My Soul

Poetry for me is like a masquerade ball, where you or Cinderella can leave your glass slipper or loafer at the top of the stairs, and no one can find you unless you want to be found. Yet, you have the maneuverability to go back to your life as a stay at home mom, a teacher, a corporate executive, or a rodeo clown. Then at the end of this manufactured fairytale, you are responsible for the happily and not so happily ever after. You have the ability to take off this invisible mask and give both voice and meaning to your work. So this is an opportunity for a true unveiling. The very depths of your soul can receive healing light to promote a certain amount of valid growth and maturity. In other words, be vulnerable to the human condition as you set yourself free. You unconsciously give others permission to be free as well.

The "Ballad, Beat, Blank Verse, Composition, Creation, Epic, Free Verse, Lyrical, Poesy, Ode, To the Lover of My Soul" came about because I felt that this piece of work wasn't just one thing, but many things rolled into one. It has dimension, character, and depth. Although it may have started out as a single seed, it has now branched off into many directions. The poetic pieces capture the very glimpses of colors refracting from my soul. In some pieces you may see purples, reds, yellows, and blues. It is left to your interpretation as to what hue you may embody with each poetic expression. I hope you enjoy saying the title over, and over, and over while the range of emotional journeys are etched into your memory banks.

Jessica Mercer

Love Letters to My Savior

By Jessica Mercer

You are my desire. You are my best day every day. The only difference is that I don't have to wake each day and reminisce on how special the previous day was. With You every day is sweeter than the day before. Just when I think I have had all I can stand, You give me all the more. You exist within me and I can't exist outside of You. You are my heaven right here on earth. You are my firsts: the first thing I think about in the morning and the first thing I think about before I go to bed at night.

I am thirsty for You. My mouth fills with the sands of separation from You. My tongue feels like sandpaper. So I take a sip from Your refreshing springs. I start to feel better. My headache eases and I no longer feel like I'm about to pass out.

I love our talks. I look forward to our conversations. I enjoy our cuddle time when I just need to be held. I am no longer filled with the desperation that comes from loneliness; I am now at a place where I am alone but not lonely. I am fully content in You, Jesus. The Spiritual connection from You is what I found myself searching for in people, in things, and even within myself. I went on an endless quest that was not fruitful until I came in contact with You.

There are days where I equate our union to conjoined twins sharing a heart. For You to have my heart completely I must die, because outside of that function I cannot coexist without You. I need You. For without You, I have no life sustaining qualities or abilities. I want to go deeper in You, because I know this can't be all.

He who exists in eternity outside the realm of time, envelope me completely as I die to myself that You may be wholly magnified within me. I am desperate for You. I will fight tooth and nail to get my portion. You see, I'm greedy for You. I am glutinous over You. I am swollen with You. I am morbidly obese. Can I fit through this door? I'm standing! Oh can my legs sustain the weight of Your glory? Please, give me more!

Vulnerable

By Jessica Mercer

God, Your vulnerability allows me to feel comfortable in my nakedness.
You show me Your love forwardly!
Shouting it from the roof tops!
You tell me You love me first.
So I don't have to wait for You to say it first.
You openly display Your hand.
I don't have to wonder how You're feeling.
This is foreign to me and my involvements in a relationship.
You throw caution to the wind and You love me even
without expecting me to love You back.
Your outpourings are verbally indescribable!
I am in awe of You.
You concern not Yourself with my humanly rejections.
You continue to love me in spite of me.
You ravish me completely to the point of slumbersome rest.
I rest in You.
I love in You.
I die in You, until I evolve in You.
Pleasurably vulnerable, nakedly abased, and capsized
In Your capacity to love me until I am down on my knees.
Calgon take me away. No, Jesus will do just
fine! AWHHHHHHHHHHHH!

Can I be Uninhibited with You?

By Jessica Mercer

To remove all inhibitions.
To be vulnerable.
Willingly naked and unashamed.
Open sores.
Gaping wounds.
The tenderness of my bruises,
Black,
Purple,
Blue,
Red,
Pink,
And then my skin's back to brown.
For I am weak in Your sight. I am small, barely visible.
I am breaking free!
To reveal a me without borders in You!
No fencing to let me know when to stop.
The uninhibited me in You.
I am chasing You at undocumented speeds.
I rejoice with You as the music of Your dance takes me away.
I can't be shy in You, for You are me and I am you.
How silly would it be to be coy with myself, to withdraw into, to
retreat into, a shell created by the enemy who is no friend of me?
Boldly in Your presence,
I stand tall and uninhibited.
He who knows of no inhibitions, Jesus!

Unemployed, Will Work for Love

By Jessica Mercer

I was desperate.
My heart was in a state of unemployment.
I was looking for love even if it was part-time.
I didn't care if I had no benefits and was being paid under the table.
I just wanted some money in my pocket.

This currency of love.
I found myself doing everything and just about anything
To keep from what I thought to be emotionally bankrupt.
It really didn't matter; your husband, your boyfriend,
your girlfriend, your wife, and even me.

I was desperate.
At the end of the day, I was no closer to finding what I needed.
I pounded that pavement for love with a sign
around my neck "will work for love."
I would get a few scraps here or there, but nothing life sustaining.
Because at the end of the night, they always went home
and I was always left alone with my thoughts.
Because they always took more than they gave.

Then I met You.
A full-time job that took me from the heap of those
burning oranges or were they tangerines?
You gave me garments of scarlet and robes of purple royalty.
You bathed me in hyssop and anointed my head with oil.
You washed my feet, yet I should have been
the one with the alabaster box.
You cleaned away the grime and the filth
that was clinging to my very soul.
You gave me rest and sprinkled my body with new mercies.
I was desperate for You, but I am no longer who I was.

I am desperate for You, lover of my soul.
I am a recipient of full-time benefits in You.
Christ, full-time employment, full-time
benefits, and no experience necessary.
Open for business

When Thoughts are Broken, Where Do They Go to Mend?

By Jessica Mercer

Do they go to the fix-it shop?
Are they taken in for repairs?
If so, where?
How are they mended?
Father, will You renew my mind to assemble my broken thoughts?
With my mind fixed on You,
Like a child never wanting to leave the ocean, not even to
eat. Like a child, my fingers are pruney and my body is
chilled. But yet, I never want to leave this place of rest.
For my thoughts soar in revelations of You.
The renewal of my mind.
The regeneration of my thoughts.
The mending of brokenness is Your specialty as You
repair not only thoughts, but hearts, minds, souls,
spirits, and anything that stands in disrepair.
The irreplaceable and undeniable one-stop shop!
Jesus, open for business!

Rejected People Reject People

By Jessica Mercer

I'm sorry.
I'm scared.
I reject you before you reject me. Tag you're it!
Can't hurt me when I hurt you first!
Nothing invested. Nothing to lose.
Everybody goes. Nobody stays.
What are you still doing here?
Space!
No space between us!
When you reject me, you reject you.
My heart.
I'm falling and I know what it is to be broken!
Stop!
Don't stop!
I don't want to be hurt when you stop loving me.
My heart's invested, but my mind keeps reminding me
that rejection leaves a bad taste in your mouth.
If one more person walks out that door,
Dry bones.
I am what!
Ashes to ashes dust to dust.
Clay!
Mold me as this residue of rejection dissipates.
Restored!
Jesus!

Where Are You?

By Jessica Mercer

Where are You?
No, where are you?
Is what I hear ringing in my head.
Where are you?
What do You mean?
I'm right here.
No, where are you?
There has been a disconnect. I see you but I don't feel you.
Sin. Separation. Backslidden state.
Where are you?
Going through the motions?
Where are you?
Preaching in the pulpit.
I'm just going through the motions of my sins.
Lord knows, it won't happen again!
Filthy rags!
Yet I am redeemed, bought with a price.
I repent!
Thank God for saving my life!
Where are you?
Because God can save you too!
No longer wrapped, no longer clothed, no longer laced in sin.
Divided as far as the east is from the west. No sin, but forgiven.
A-M-E-N

Failures

By Jessica Mercer

My failures in life don't equate to my failures in Christ.
He's on a different grading system.
For we count it a loss to lose life.
But He says that if you lose your life, you will gain a life.
We count it a loss to lose earthly treasures, but in
Christ our treasures don't lie in earthen vessels.
He's on a different grading system.
"Wherefore I put thee in remembrance that thou stir up the gift
of God which is in thee by the putting on of my hands.
For God hath not given us the spirit of fear; but of
power and of love and of a sound mind"
(II Timothy 1:6).

Sparrow

By Jessica Mercer

I hear what sounds like a thousand birds chirping outside of my window.
It sounds more like a billion fingernails being
clawed down a blackboard all at once.
I imagine they are a family coming home at the end of the day,
conversing about the comings and goings of their day.
In the chirpings there are highs and lows, almost as if
someone told a joke and they're all laughing at once.
How is it that even birds know that regardless of
the triumphs and failures, at the end of the day all
that matters are those you started out with?
"Dear God, make me a bird so that I can fly far, far, away!"
So at the end of the day, I will always know where to nest.
Comfort in the warmth of Your wings and
the shine of the sun to my back.
To be as close to heaven as God would allow, as I
soar above things that are greater than I.
So I won't seem so small in the world.
To find solace in the clouds. From that
distance I cast an enormous shadow.
So instead of a sparrow, I resemble an eagle.
But does that make me less than or greater than, or perhaps
temporarily more than who I may actually be?
Dear God, I changed my mind. Make me into me and
allow the change of me within be into You. So I am as
great or as humble as You would allow me to be.
Because at the end of the day, my nest is to rest within Your arms.

The Greatness Within

By Jessica Mercer

Assuredly, He tells me I am great.
Not in a whisper, but in an audible tone.
Letting me know His words were no mistake.
Like a baby bird in its nest, I flex my wings.
The bird takes a flying leap from its nest.
This time the ground instead of the wind
catches its blunder in the way of a fall.
Mother knows best.
Let's try again, for once is not enough.

I am created for the greatness within!
Like a rainbow trout who innately knows how to swim.
It flounders in the currents, smashing upon the rocks it was spawned in.
I am created for the greatness within!
An eagle soars above the clouds.
Its nest rests in the cliffs of mountains.
Yet its wings dance in the twilight of gazing stars.
Who flies above the head of this king of birds
but the sun, the moon, and the stars?
Yet its perch is at the cusp of extinction.

I am created for the greatness within!
As a gazelle takes graceful strides across the
African plain with wind at its rapid feet,
Away it gallops from gnashing teeth.

I am created for the greatness within!
Once the ugly duckling is hatched from its fragile shell,
Awkwardly unattractive it takes a step.
Whether it recognizes it today or some other day,
It was created for the immeasurable beauty of a swan.

As I am created for the greatness within regardless
of the wrapping I was born in.
Because not only I, but you were created for the greatness within! Selah.

A Child's Heart

By Jessica Mercer

I breathe You in and hold my breath until I pass out!
The thought of having to release to let You go disturbs me.
The street lights are on and I'm not ready for our play time to end.
My mother's calling with her foot tapping on the porch.
"Don't worry," You say, "I will see you first thing in the morning."
You are my most favorite thing on any given day;
forget my blankey, my dolly, and my bike!
You are my everlasting guiding light!
We play hide-n-go-seek all day as You jump out as I have found You!
I am rewarded with You!
You are the prize of the high calling.
You are my greatest reward.
For You sit on the mantle of my heart, a trophy for my soul!
He who fades, not!

Your Grace is Sufficient

By Jessica Mercer

I thank you Lord for Your sufficient grace as I war against my flesh.
I thank you Lord God for the strength that You have equipped me
with as I beat my flesh into submission and as I resist feeding this
thing inside of me. I deny myself the pleasure of pleasuring myself,
my urges, my impulses, and my needs to pleasure myself, I abuse me
so I won't abuse others. But it is worse, I think to abuse me because
my guilt is internalized. To sin against my very soul. A coup, an
uprising within as my flesh, tries to gain control over my soul.
I thank you Lord God for Your sufficient grace. As You replace my
bloodline curse of lust and incest with Your grace and mercy. How
do I have mercy for my soul when my flesh would rather see me
burn? Grace and mercy to the rescue: God's dynamic superheroes.
So Lord, make my weapon sharp as iron, for iron sharpeneth iron.
May the flames be hot as You crucify my flesh. Because there is
no separation between us, even if it is I that is in the way!
May my weapons pierce my flesh that is the enemy to my soul.
No friend of me is of me.
Mommy said, "be careful of strangers," but my
greatest adversaries I have always known.
I thank you Lord God, for Your grace is sufficient. I thank you Lord
God for seeing the residue that was left behind. Thank you Lord God
for placing me under the knife for that last surgery in this area of my
life. The enemy knew it was time to go. We have been in this eviction
process for quite some time, going back and forth to court for the
rights to my soul. You accuser of the brethren! You pulled out all the
stops of distraction to keep me out of focus. You used my finances,
my family, men of interest, and even me to hinder your moving day.
You have been locked out of what you thought was your home. A
sticker declares in bold red letters "final eviction." Your stuff, your
junk, and your crap have been exposed to the curb. Your lies are out
in the open, your hate, your wiles, your deceit, your trickery, and your
defeat. I would continue to pick through your mess, but not anymore;
I know it all too well. It's time for you to find someplace else to live!

Can't Fall Asleep if the TV Ain't On

By Jessica Mercer

Street light streams through the darkness of the kitchen brighter than the
spotlight in a jail house prison.
Can't fall asleep if the TV ain't on.
A blue-black, shirtless thief slitheringly approaches.
With no sack on his back, yet a robber none-the-less.

Can't fall asleep if the TV ain't on.
Close your eyes, say a prayer.
Now open your eyes.
Oh, he's still there. So much for prayer.
Closer comes the boogey man.
I told my mama he was real!

Can't fall asleep if the TV ain't on.
I close my eyes tighter and hold my breath.
This four-way intersection flashes red all at once.
Impatient green lights, sound of collisions, horns, crashes in my head.

Can't fall asleep if the TV ain't on.
Four to a bunk. He ain't no punk. His eyes aren't set on me!
A pirate's booty, he does not take.
But the beauty of a virgin's chastity belt was his prize.

Can't fall asleep if the TV ain't on, 'cause surely if it's on, he won't come
back.................BOO!
Can't fall asleep if the TV ain't on.

This Cocoon of Singleness

By Jessica Mercer

Shielded in this cocoon of singleness.
Wrapped in the virtues of womanhood.
A platform for my Esther or my Baby Ruth, wrapped into my Naomi training.

Whoso findeth a wife findeth a good thing.
Well, where is he looking?
Feeling like a jack-in-the-box waiting to be found.
"All around the mulberry bush the monkey chased the weasel. The monkey said it's all in fun.
Pop!" Just checking to see if the door's still working. "Goes the weasel!"

So many liberators tarrying at my door. None of them has the right key to unlock this door.
Satisfied in my singleness, I think I'll wait a bit more.
Until Jesus gives flight to my wings folded in this cocoon of singleness.

"Butterfly in the sky, I can fly twice as high."
On the wings of marriage given flight through Christ.
This cocoon of singleness, interrupted.

"Psych your mind, make your booty shine!"
It was all a dream of marriage.
A place of habitation in my hibernation, this cocoon of singleness to be continued......

Don't Let Me Fall Asleep

By Jessica Mercer

Complete exhaustion, my slumber's rest.
Hiding from my nightmares' endings.
I have to say I stay awake to escape the darkness of rest
That has me gasping for my breath.

Falling back to sleep in a nightmare of my realities.
By far, running dreams are the worst!
As Mama says, "The devil's chasing you."
Now it's time to pray. Now I lay me down to sleep. I pray the Lord my
soul to keep.

But how do you keep from falling into a sleep?
Remembering that which you thought you put to rest.
A nail in that coffin buried in your mental chest, languished in unrest at
the distress of your blockages.

In the dreams and visions of the night, as deep sleep falleth upon men
slumbering in their beds.
He openeth ears of men, sealing their instruction.
To withdraw them from their purpose and their pride.
Kept souls from tasting the very pits of hell.

The only nails that matter were in His hands and His feet, with a crown
of thorns: no need to repeat.
Cast your cares to His delight, for His yolk is easy and His burdens are
light.

Swirly

By Jessica Mercer

Don't want to be left with the thoughts that swirl around in my head.
Imposing thoughts that come around, not giddy or embracing.
Thoughts of blue skies and rainbows don't come to mind.

The volume is high to break up my thoughts.
The volume is low so I can rest in my thoughts.
Always busy, around me, sounds filling spaces to hide the cracks that run in straight lines.

Hiding from this mental attack, thoughts that swirl around in my head.
I hear the most when things are quiet.
Even silence has sound.
That white noise from a channel that has gone to sleep for the night.

Thoughts that swirl around in my head.
Catching up to me like the women running from nothing with heels that always seems to break.
A psychotic break. A movie in slow motion right before it burns.
Renew the mind of the thoughts that swirl around in my head.

Spiritual Antibodies

By Jessica Mercer

No one knows you better than yourself.
No one knows your formation better than Christ.
No one knows your flaws better than the enemy that would try to put an end to me.

I wonder if spiritual antibodies grow inside a Petri dish in heaven's lab.
Angels in lab coats focusing on folks that have the worst case of sin.
Sin, the cancer of pious living.

The cure is a dose of Christ taken as frequently as needed. No drug interactions or dosage restrictions.
Spiritual antibodies against this fleshly condition, human condition, lustful condition, self-centered condition, impatient condition, etc. Can someone get the Great Physician?
From sin, a saved survivor trying to avoid a relapse into a sinful recap.

Heaven's pharmaceuticals: joy unspeakable, Balm in Gilead healing creams, peace beyond understanding chews, and eternal life shakes.
Hell's placebos: sinful joy bars, lusty elixirs, anger caplets, and death juice.

No need for HMOs or PPOs or shelves packed with this drug trying to counteract that drug.
But one bottle of Christ will combat whatever ails ya! Money back guaranteed!

Light! Light! Light!

By Jessica Mercer

We are the light in dark places.
Does that mean if you're not casting light, you're a shadow?

Ye are the light of the world.
Cities set on hills cannot be hidden.

We are beacons.
We are lighthouses.
We are search lights that cut through shadows.

Are we bulbs that heaven replaces, tapping the top so the light won't stop?
Death quenches earthen radiance, but spiritual resplendence is displaced.
So as souls are saved, there are instances of bursting lights that would make pyrotechnics blush.
As we flush out the darkness that has no place in light.

So from above, we are illuminations of soulful beacons, lighthouses, searchlights, flashlights, fog lights, hazard lights, match lights, headlights, moonlights, sun lights, twilights, sparkling lights, nightlights, warm lights, some light!

Are you casting a shadow or light?
"Let your light so shine before men, that they may see your good works, and glorify your Father which is in heaven."

I Never Thought I'd feel This Way Before

By Jessica Mercer

I never thought I'd feel this way before; my heart is open and so is yours.
I gave my heart so many times before, but it was tossed aside and smashed
on the floor.
I used to think that if I gave him my body, it would keep him from walking
out that door.
But now I know what it means to truly be loved.
The love from my heavenly Father above, for we know that God is love.

I never thought I'd feel this way before; my heart is open and so is yours.
The enemy would have you to think that there is no God up above.
But he is a liar, and God is the creator of love.
He loved me before I was formed in my mother's womb.

I never thought I'd feel this way before; my heart is open and so is yours.
Our God paid the ultimate price with His son Jesus' life.
I never thought I'd feel this way before, but I found love in Jesus Christ.

My First Time

By Jessica Mercer

I had my first French kiss when I was only three.
For you see, he was not much older than me and we shared the same tree.

I had my first introduction to a lesbian escapade when I was only five.
For you see, she was much older than me and we shared the same pedigree.

I had my first petting by this boy named................
Since when do we do names while we are playing games on the jungle gym in kindergarten?
I told her that he was touching me, but "Go play," she said, "Stop disturbing me."

I had my first seduction while laying flat on the beige and cream-tiled floor.
"I'll do anything," were the last words I said as I entered the boy's bathroom door with my head under the sink. Shamefaced was I behind a red He-Man backpack that covered up my face, while exposing the remorse that soaked into my skin.

I had my first deflowering when I was..................
I'm tired of these firsts, so let me leave while I have at least one sleeve to cry into, for these are my first times.

Trust

By Jessica Mercer

I know every intimate relationship you've had ended in hurt.
You have shied away from intimacy, because you don't want to recall the bittersweet taste of rejection.
You get close to intimacy and then you shy away.

I need you to know that you can trust Me with your secrets.
I have not come to hurt you.
I only want the best for you, My daughter.

Please leave behind distrust and your past intimate rejections.
This is hindering our relationship.
I can only get as close as you allow, stop shutting Me out.

I won't force myself on you like those men of your past.
I will go only as far as you allow me to.
I will wait on you.
Don't keep Me at arm's length.
Take Me in close, cheek to cheek, breast to breast.

Steal Away

By Jessica Mercer

I steal away to Your presence,
As a host steals away from her
Guests to absorb the capacity of the evening.

I steal away to Your presence,
Like a thief in the night that has
Stolen an enthusiastic bounty under
The cover of darkness.

I steal away to Your presence,
That would absorb the essence
Of being in Your presence one more time.

I steal away to Your presence.
Like an addict clothed in addiction,
I would leave my bed, my family, my job
To have a hit of Your remnants.

I steal away to Your presence.
Just a closer walk with Thee; grant it, Jesus, is my plea,
Daily walking close to Thee, let it be, dear Lord, let it be.

I steal away to Your presence,
As a child escapes from the warmth of her bed
To exchange the warmth of her parents' pillow.

I steal away to Your presence,
Escaping with the restraints of time because with You
Every millisecond multiplies into hours, and hours into months,
And months into millennium.
A loss of seconds in Your presence,
A day in Thy presence is better than a thousand, as
I steal away to Your presence that resides in You.

He Who Cannot be Contained

By Jessica Mercer

153

He who cannot be contained!
Not by words.
Not by this world.
Not by the spiritual.
Not by the metaphysical.

He who cannot be contained!
The indescribable.
The palatable.
The increase.

He who cannot be contained!
Yet praise.
Yet deliverance.
Yet! Yet! Yet!
He who cannot be contained!

What I Feel

By Sandra Barnes

This is what I feel…
Friendliness from the warmth of a gentle smile,
Intimacy bonded by trust of an innocent child.
Suspicion that impregnates an opposing team,
Betrayal when truth uncovers a manipulative scheme.
FORGIVENESS is what I feel, because without it, I cannot heal.

This is what I feel…
Anger burning like a passionate rage,
Fear trapping my soul in a fastened cage.
Guilt stabbing painful memories of every mistake,
Shame forcing an insidious image of self-hate.
I feel the beauty of **GRACE,** *covering a past that cannot be erased.*

This is what I feel…
Anxiety whose grip renders immobility,
Worry robbing my mental capacity.
Confusion and its chaotic grip pushing me toward insanity,
Frustration blinding reality.
PEACE is what I feel when I release the world, and in silence, sit still.

This is what I feel…
Doubt casting a shadow over my mind,
Disappointment from a dream snatched and declined.
Grief emptying my heart, leaving it hollow,
Restoration filling my spirit, replacing the sorrow.
My soul He will appease, and in His Comfort, I feel at **ease.**

This is what I feel…
Hope for what tomorrow will bring,
Belief that God created all living things.
Love for the Spirit abiding in me,
Joy for what He created me to be.

And in the midst of each emotion, His presence is revealed.
*So in **everything that I feel, I still know that He is real.***

S I X

LOVE LETTERS

Imagine being able to express yourself from your Mother's womb as you anticipate your debut into the world. The excitement builds, then suddenly fear kicks in. Imagine the feeling of desperation when it becomes clear that you may never get to meet the amazing woman that would be your everything in life. Journey with me as I express my thoughts, feelings and most of all…my love, to my Momma.

-*Al Collins*

Dear Momma,

So the doctor said you couldn't have children. Silly Rabbit. God knew all about me before I was ever here in your womb. Doctors always think they've got the answer, and sometimes they do, but not this time Momma, not this time.

You see, I know you've been in your closet every day, praying for the child God promised you. Praying that he or she would be healthy and most of all would love you unconditionally as you would love him or her. I know you used to babysit all of the neighborhood kids and as you watched them play and grow, you longed for one of your own, promising God that you would give any and everything to be blessed with a child. Promising that you would sacrifice your life for your child, if He would just give you the gift of becoming a mother.

In that closet, you heard God promise that He would answer your prayers. From the moment you heard His confirmation, you believed – you trusted in His word. No doctor or anybody else could take away His promise. You know that He is a God that cannot lie. So once you got the promise, you simply had to wait for Him to tell you when to expect your miracle.

I know you got anxious and would still go to your closet. "God, I know You promised me a child, but when? When will he or she be here? Have You forgotten me, God? I'm waiting. I'm waiting. Do You hear me, God?"

At some point you stopped asking. You didn't give up, but you knew so desperately in your heart that He would fulfill His promise.

In the meantime, your father got sick and went to Heaven. You put your whole self into grieving for him. You were the youngest child and always felt closer to him than the others. Thomas Fleming Kinney. He had a lot on his plate. He had a large family to care for. He worked hard and I think I heard Grandma say he played hard, too – whatever that means. But he always made time for you, his Alma. So his death touched your heart in a way so different from your siblings. You loved him more, so you missed him more. Right, momma?

After the funeral you were weak with emotions, not only from Grandpa Tom's death, but from comforting Grandma. She was grieving too, and needed you, her youngest, to comfort her.
When you got home, Daddy was there for you. You talked; you cried and from the love you shared, your promise from God was conceived.

When the nausea and back pains persisted, you knew, you knew, you knew! You shouted even before you made the appointment with the doctor. He immediately told you he'd see you but there must have been something else wrong, because it was impossible for you to be pregnant. As he looked at the test he said, while shaking his head and looking over his glasses – "Impossible! Impossible! You're pregnant!" And you gave him that "I know, 'cause God told me so" look. Impossible? Who made up that word, Momma? I hope you never try to teach me that word. If you do, I just won't listen. Grandma always says, "All things are possible if you believe in Jesus Christ," and I'm going to believe in Him - I just know it!

After telling Daddy about me, the next person to tell was Grandma. She had her own prayer closet and prayed day and night. I couldn't always hear what she was saying but I just know it was about me. So my imminent arrival was not a surprise to her. She promised to always be with you and care for you and your child. The painful void for both of you that was now there from Granddaddy's death would now be filled by God's wonderful blessing of what was to be your one and only child.

Thank you, Momma, for believing God's word and for not believing the doctor's report.

I love you,
Your one and only daughter

Dear Momma,

I know it's been a long pregnancy – the doctor told you I'd be arriving by September and here it is October and I'm not ready yet. But whenever my arrival is scheduled, it will be just as God planned and right on time. I've heard you say that He's an on-time God. Isn't that what you said, Momma?

Hold on, Momma. I know your feet are swollen and you've gained a lot of weight. You've gained how much? Wow! That's a lot. Don't worry, I'll help you lose the weight. We're a team. Hold on Momma. I'm coming. It won't be long now.

I love you,
Your one and only daughter

Dear Momma,

Okay, seems like the doctor is wrong again. Silly Rabbit! It's November and God hasn't given me the go ahead yet. I'm sorry. I know I keep turning and kicking, but it's getting a little uncomfortable for me too. I want to come out and meet you and Daddy. And I really want to meet this lady that I'm going to call Grandma. She seems like a feisty little "don't take no stuff from nobody" woman. She's my kind of woman. I hope I'm a lot like her.

Okay, I'm turning again – I'm turning. Oh my goodness, I've turned completely around. Oh no! My feet are going to come out first. Oh no! God, turn me around again! I don't want to hurt my Momma! I'm sorry, Momma. My feet are going to come out first! Help me!!

What's that the doctor just said? They're going to try and turn me around? I don't know about this momma, I hope it works because I don't want to cause you any more pain. I love you! I love you!

A "C" section. What's that? Wait! Don't cut my Momma!! I'll turn around – God, where are you?

What's that he just said? You're not going to make it? Does that mean you're going to die? Tell the doctor he's wrong! If you're not going to make it, I don't want to make it either. We're a team! We've been through a lot together. Grandma, Daddy – where are you? – do something!!!

I love you,
Your one and only daughter

Dear God,

Please don't let my Momma die. If You can't come here Yourself, please send Your angels to help us. I know You didn't bring her this far to leave her. Could it be that You promised her a child, but You didn't promise her she'd be around to see me? Who's going to teach me about You, who's going to dress me in pretty clothes and comb my hair, who's going to take me to school on my first day and who's going to come to my piano recitals? I know Grandma and Daddy will take care of me, but I need my Momma. God please send the angels to save my Momma. I love her!!

Dear Momma,

Okay, I'm here. I think this is a blanket I'm in. Is that you holding me, Momma? Okay, whew!!! We made it!

Momma, I heard you ask the doctor where were all of the beautiful nurses, glowing in beautiful flowing white gowns who surrounded your bed and told you that we were going to be okay. The doctor gave you a puzzled look and replied that there had never been a group of nurses surrounding your bed. God had answered my prayer and sent His angels. Beautiful angels, shining in God's glory, were sent to comfort you, Momma. Thank you, God, for saving my Momma.

I love you,
Your one and only daughter

Dear Momma,

We're home!!! What's that name you're calling me? Alma? Alma?? What kind of name is that?? Oh wait a minute – they're calling you that name too!! I thought your name was Momma. Well, Momma is what I'm going to call you. Why on earth would they call us Alma?

Okay – I understand. Grandma was supposed to put my name on my birth certificate as Albemarle but she decided to name me Alma. I'm not sure which one is worse. But I think I came out on top with Alma. But can you imagine how the kids in school are going to butcher my name – they'll call me Elma, Elmer Fudd, Alma Jr., and who knows what else. So why give me that name? Okay – I understand. When Grandma thought you were going to die giving birth to me, she wanted your child to carry on your name. Okay, got it. So, who's going to answer when they say Alma – you or me? Never mind, I know you will figure it out. Actually, we'll figure it out together. We'll figure everything out together, because we're a team.

I love you,
Your one and only daughter

My mother peacefully went home to be with the Lord on June 12, 2010. She was 91 years old. God promised her a child and I am so grateful that He chose me. I will always love and miss you, Momma.

Lighthouse

By: LaShawn Gardner

The sun and moon pass by while you remain there,

Providing light to those who enter your space.

Servicing as a safe place of refuge,

Those who embrace you will find strength.

I was overtaken by the wind.

Emerged in darkness as far and wide as the waters extend.

But you searched for me,

Far beyond the depths of my deserving.

Relentlessly searching as if I belonged to you.

Your light shone upon my face reflecting my faults across the waters.

Exposing me to your commandment,

While sparing me from judgement.

I had fallen into the deepest part of the raging sea,

Drowning under anger, submerged by hatred

I was unrecognizable to the ones that called me daughter.

And I deserved to stay there,

But your light brought life to the darkness that had overtaken.

It extended its reach and pulled me to dry land,

Reviving my body with a fresh wind.

It planted my feet upon the sand.

Your light brought my life to safety.

The raging waters were now behind me,

And there in the distance was everything new.

And I never had to wonder who saved me,

I knew it was you.

ABOUT THE AUTHORS: BIOGRAPHIES

Rev. Katrina Wallace was born and raised in the Washington, D.C. metropolitan area. She attended Bowie State University and received a Bachelor of Science Degree in Psychology, graduating Magna Cum Laude. She was licensed in ministry in 1994 and ordained as an Associate Pastor in 2004. She currently serves as the Assistant Director of the Counseling Ministry and as a Life Direction's Sunday School Teacher to women at Cornerstone Peaceful Bible Church, where Rev. Daniel and Sabrina Mangrum are the senior pastors.

Additionally, Katrina is a school Guidance Counselor for grades K3 – 12th and serves as the chaplain of Excellence Christian School. She is blessed to be married to her wonderful husband, Robert Wallace and God has blessed them with two lovely children, Charity Royale and Emmanuel Edward Wallace. It is Katrina's desire to serve God wholeheartedly, reflecting His nature as a citizen of the Kingdom.

Rev. Letrice Weaver was born and raised in Washington, D.C., where she attended Howard University and received a Bachelor of Business Administration degree in Marketing. She has written over 30 inspirational poems and was blessed to recently publish her first book, _An Invitation From the King_. In May of 1996, she accepted her call into public ministry and was later licensed as a minister of the gospel at Cornerstone Peaceful Bible Baptist Church (CPBBC). In 2004, she was ordained as one of the Associate Pastors at CPBBC and currently serves as a Women's

Sunday School Teacher, an Intercessory Prayer Ministry Leader and Communications Ministry Leader. Rev. Letrice loves God with all of her heart and desires to be an instrument that God can use to empower others to walk in God's plan for their lives. One of her deepest and most heartfelt desires is to see the people of God, especially women, set free from the bondages of fear, insecurity and low self-esteem, of which she is a living testimony. Rev. Letrice and her husband, Todd Weaver, reside in Clinton, MD with their two beautiful children, Letaria Renee and Todd Anthony, II.

Ms. Jessica Mercer grew up in a small town in North Carolina, where she was able to practice her oratory and writing skills, and win a few local contests. She is no stranger to writing, although this is her first co-authored published work. When Jessica was in the first grade, she entered her first poetry contest for a greeting card company. At around fourteen years old, she attempted her first romance novel, but quickly realized a fourteen-year old did not know enough about love to fill a book. However, she was really good at making things up. After Jessica graduated from high school, she joined the great migration part two from the south, went to Howard University for a few semesters, and settled into the southern Maryland area.

Rev. Lesley Poole has been a member of Cornerstone Peaceful Bible Baptist Church since 1998, when she moved from California to help open the Nation's first urban public college preparatory boarding school. Lesley accepted Christ in her senior year of high school and joined Campus Crusade for Christ in college. There she developed a thirst for God's word, evangelism, and a heart for praise and worship. Her walk with God has brought deep deliverance and a heart to forgive others as she's been forgiven. At Cornerstone, she serves as a new members' class teacher and servant leader for the Hands of Excellence sign language ministry.

Lesley is one of The SEED School of Washington, D.C.'s founding faculty members and is the incoming CEO for The SEED Foundation. For 18 years, she held positions ranging from Principal, Director of Admissions to Director of Parent & Community Relations, Director of Student Life, and Director of Outreach and Chief growth and policy.

Rather working at SEED or Cornerstone, it is all about serving for Lesley. It's her heart's desire that her life would be an offering to all those God places in her life. Her life's scripture is II Timothy 2:2, "And the [instructions] which you have heard from me along with many witnesses, transmit and entrust [as a deposit] to reliable and faithful men who will be competent and qualified to teach others also."

Mrs. Ardener Taylor Lott was born in Henderson, NC, and raised in Southeastern Pennsylvania. As a child, she fell in love with books and writing, and continues in adulthood to indulge in the pleasures of both. She was saved by grace at the age of twelve at the Second Baptist Church of Wayne, PA. She attended the University of Pittsburgh where she obtained a BA, followed by a M.Ed. from Eastern College in Saint Davids, PA. She is a teacher at heart and enjoys the company of children over adults! She attributes her successes to the grace, mercy, and blessings of The Most High God! Among those blessings, she counts her mother and role model, Sandra Rachel Montague, her husband and best friend, Pastor Fred Lott, Jr., and her children and greatest teachers Gabriella, Dominique, Josiah, and Donalson. She is a transplanted resident of Lake Wylie, SC, where she works as a church administrator, teachers' assistant, and domestic engineer of her home, Grace Manor. Her favorite scripture verses are Proverbs 3:5-6.

Rev. Al Collins was licensed in ministry in 2010 and served as an Associate Minister at Cornerstone Peaceful Bible Baptist Church, where her Pastors were Daniel and Sabrina Mangrum. She currently serves as Worship Leader Chair and ministers the word of God at Bells United Methodist Church in Camp Springs, Maryland. Minister Al and her husband Michael also serve on the leadership team at Bells, under the direction of Rev. Johnsie Cogman. Additionally, Minister Al is a certified life coach, professional inspirational speaker, and public speaking and communication skills trainer. Minister Al and her husband Michael are parents of six adult children and are blessed to have 16 grandchildren and 4 great grandchildren. They reside in Cheltenham, Maryland.

FEATURED WRITERS

Sandra Barnes

Rev. Daniel T. Mangrum

Shawnta Nelson

Elbie Williams, Jr.

Alkeisha L. Williams

LaShawn Gardner

ACKNOWLEDGMENTS

I wish to express my sincere gratitude to all the co-authors and featured writers that contributed to this project. I would like to especially thank the Editors, Gretel Coverdale and Andrea Nelson, for their time and diligence dedicated to the editorial review.

Additionally, I would like to thank my pastor Rev. Daniel T. Mangrum for his contribution to this project and note that he has an outstanding published book entitled, "Crossover Changes" that is a life changing manuscript for all who wish to indulge. Furthermore, I would like to note that Rev. Letrice Weaver has a published book entitled "An Invitation from the King" and Rev. Al Collins has published work entitled, "My Sister's Journey."

I would be remiss if I didn't thank my beloved husband and beautiful daughter for allowing me to share my heart for poetry with them from time to time. Their willingness to enter my world of poetry and embrace my passion is greatly appreciated.

The ladies that I co-authored with on this project are my sisters in Christ as well as my friends. I thank God for them and I thank God for the work that He performed in us as we sometimes travailed to birth some of the writings shared in this project.

To God Be All the Glory!!!